THE SECRET LIFE OF STORIES

Michael Bérubé

THE SECRET LIFE OF STORIES

From Don Quixote
to Harry Potter,
How Understanding
Intellectual Disability
Transforms the Way We Read

NEW YORK UNIVERSITY PRESS

New York and London

NEW YORK UNIVERSITY PRESS
New York and London
www.nyupress.org

© 2016 by New York University
All rights reserved

References to Internet websites (URLs) were accurate at the time of writing. Neither the author nor New York University Press is responsible for URLs that may have expired or changed since the manuscript was prepared.

ISBN: 978-1-4798-2361-1

For Library of Congress Cataloging-in-Publication data, please contact the Library of Congress.

New York University Press books are printed on acid-free paper, and their binding materials are chosen for strength and durability. We strive to use environmentally responsible suppliers and materials to the greatest extent possible in publishing our books.

Manufactured in the United States of America

10 9 8 7 6 5 4 3 2 1

Also available as an ebook

In memory of Anne Clarke Bérubé

(1935–2013)

We live immersed in narrative, recounting and reassessing the meaning of our past actions, anticipating the outcome of our future projects, situating ourselves at the intersection of several stories not yet completed. The narrative impulse is as old as our oldest literature: myth and folktale appear to be stories we recount in order to explain and understand where no other form of explanation will work. The desire and the competence to tell stories also reach back to an early stage in the individual's development, to about the age of three, when a child begins to show the ability to put together a narrative in coherent fashion and especially the capacity to recognize narratives, to judge their well-formedness. Children quickly become virtual Aristotelians, insisting upon any storyteller's observation of the "rules," upon proper beginnings, middles, and particularly ends.

—Peter Brooks, *Reading for the Plot*

CONTENTS

ACKNOWLEDGMENTS

Many thanks to Phyllis Eisenson Anderson, Christopher Robinson, and Susan Squier for reading this book in manuscript almost as soon as it was written; thanks also to Chris Castiglia, Chris Reed, and Anne McCarthy, dear colleagues at Penn State, for reading the "Motive" chapter as part of our collaborative writing group. A special thanks to Richard Powers, for reading the manuscript with painstaking care and for not minding my line about Western Union in my brief discussion of his 2006 novel *The Echo Maker*. My colleagues in disability studies have been discussing bits and pieces of this book as I have stitched them together over the years, and I need especially to thank hosts and interlocutors at the University of Missouri, Syracuse University, the University of Louisville, George Washington University, Loyola University of Chicago, Duquesne University, Yale University, and the University of Virginia for allowing me to test these ideas in public forums. Closer to home, I want to thank the wonderful students of my spring 2013 graduate seminar and fall 2013 senior seminar at Penn State for working with me on some of the novels discussed in this book. Students who contributed key insights are individually thanked in the notes.

I owe a special debt to Amanda Anderson and the School for Criticism and Theory at Cornell University—and to my participants in the summer 2013 seminar, "Narrative, Intellectual Disability and the Boundaries of the Human." People who have been through SCT's six-week summer program often describe it as a transformative intellectual experience, and now I know why. It was the most rigorous and rewarding six weeks of my professional life. I want to thank all my seminar participants for putting up with the examples of "evocriticism" I asked them to read, which exasperated some of them no end; more substantially, I want to thank Sandra Danilovic, Andrew Ferguson, Leon Hilton, Brandon Jones, Péter Makai, Kate Noson, David Oswald, Conor Pitetti, Michael Sawyer, and Jess Waggoner for sustained exchanges that continue to this day. My fellow seminar leaders, Ian Baucom, Jane Bennett, and Julia Reinhard Lupton, were whip-smart and relentlessly witty, and the marathon one-hour question/answer periods after every lecture, combined with the two-hour dissection of each seminar leader's work, are things I will remember for as long as I have memories. Presiding over it all, Amanda Anderson was brilliant and gracious—as usual.

Portions of this book have been previously published in *PMLA*, *American Scientist*, the *Blackwell Companion to American Literary Studies*, and the *Common Review*.

This is the first scholarly book whose contents I have discussed not only with my older son, Nicholas, but also with my younger son, Jamie. Jamie is aware that he has a disability, and he has been to many of my lectures and a few of my classes on disability studies (after one of which, on the history of deafness, he asked, "Am I deaf?"—thinking, as he explained, of all the audiology exams he underwent as a child). But he is even more keenly aware of disability in the world around him, and now peppers me with questions as to which characters in literature and film can plausibly be said to have disabilities.

Thank you, Jamie, for being such an observant and inquisitive young man, and thank you, Nick, for being such a perspicacious and quick-witted old man. And Janet Lyon, who shaped these ideas during every waking moment of our lives together, and possibly through much mumbling in our sleep as well: thank you for all your amazing work on literature and disability. You know your book will leave no aspect of modernist studies untouched.

My mother, Anne Clarke Bérubé, makes a brief appearance in the introduction; this book is dedicated to her memory. Here, I just want to thank her and my father, Maurice Ralph Bérubé, for helping me learn how to read and write.

State College, Pennsylvania

Introduction

Stories

Representations of disability are ubiquitous, far more prevalent and pervasive than (almost) anybody realizes. Not because of the truism that we all become disabled in one way or another if we live long enough, but because disability has a funny way of popping up everywhere without announcing itself *as* disability. Everyone knows Dumbo as the plucky little elephant who can fly; few people think of Dumbo as a child with a disability, even though his ridiculously large ears are, for most of the film, a source of stigma and shame—so much so that the other circus elephants torment Dumbo's mother into violent madness. (She is eventually deemed a danger to herself and to others, and incarcerated in a separate circus wagon.) Everyone knows that *Total Recall* (the original version) is a campy Paul Verhoeven gorefest featuring Arnold Schwarzenegger imploring Sharon Stone, "Less do eet—move to Maas"; few people realize that the film also features workers with employment-related disabilities—namely, the mutants on Mars whose mutations were caused by inadequate protection from solar radiation. And everyone knows that the X-Men are superheroes; to date, I am the only person I know who thinks that the first X-Men film, released in 2000, spent its first twenty minutes establishing the premise that the X-Men are also gay, gifted Jewish kids with disabilities.[1]

None of these films is "about" disability in the sense that *My Left Foot* or *Rain Man* or *Away from Her* is about disability, and none of them uses the word. And, more important for my purposes in this book, none of the disabilities in these films—with the sole exception of Professor Xavier in his wheelchair—is remotely "realistic." If you were to object that (a) baby elephants actually don't come with ears so large that they constantly trip over them, or (b) Martian mutants don't really have stomachs that feature fetus-like growths with psychic powers, surely you would be missing the point. Likewise, if you were to object that the association of X-Men with disability is offensive on the grounds that actual people with disabilities cannot read minds, bend steel, or change shape, you would effectively be denying fiction one of its ancient prerogatives, that of making stuff up.

This book is about fictional disabilities. The disabilities in question are "fictional" not in the sense of the "disability masquerade" so brilliantly limned by Ellen Samuels in *Fantasies of Identification*, whereby nondisabled characters feign disability, but rather, in a sense that attends to the various *deployments* of disability in fiction. I say "deployments" (and I will use the ungainly term more than once) rather than "depictions" or "representations," because I will argue—no, I will *show*—that disability and ideas about disability can be and have been put to use in fictional narratives in ways that go far beyond any specific rendering of any disabled character or characters. Representations of disability are ubiquitous, yes, even or especially when you are not looking for them; but narrative *deployments* of disability do not confine themselves to representation. They can also be narrative strategies, devices for exploring vast domains of human thought, experience, and action. Over the course of the next three chapters, I will chart three such domains: motive, time, and self-awareness. And as you read this book, I hope that you will find that disability is indeed ubiquitous and polysemous. But more than that, I hope that by the time you finish reading this book, the arguments in it will gradually have come to seem obvious to you, or that, in some as-yet-uninvented verb tense that combines the past imperfect with the future perfect, you will have realized that you were thinking these thoughts all along. And I hope that among those thoughts will be this: The various deployments of disability I analyze here, with nothing more than the tools of close reading, are also powerful meditations on what it means to be a social being, a sentient creature with an awareness of time, mortality, causality, and sentience itself.

* * *

I chose Peter Brooks's *Reading for the Plot* for my epigraph, my inscription over the gate to this book, because I think that his are words to live by, regardless of whether you are a professional literary critic. Narrative is important because it informs everything we think, do, plan, remember, and imagine. We tell stories—and we listen to stories, and we gauge the "well-formedness" of stories—within a couple of years of learning to walk and talk. That insight has been revisited in recent years by "evocritics," or "literary Darwinists," who argue not merely that we are hardwired for storytelling (which we may well be, if our children are any indication), but also that our capacity for storytelling has survival value—it is an *adaptation*, an evolutionary contrivance that somehow got us through the Pleistocene. I will take up the claims of the evocritics in my final chapter, reading them from the perspective of disability studies (as no one has done to date); for now, to open my discussion, I want to return to the premise of Brooks's *Reading for the Plot* for more humble, personal reasons.[2] I want to start by telling you about my kids.

My kids are no longer kids. One is in his late twenties, one in his early twenties; Nick, the firstborn, was a "gifted" child, capable of copying drawings of medieval European hill cities at the age of five; Jamie, his brother, has Down syndrome. Jamie also has an encyclopedic knowledge of sharks and the music of the Beatles, as well as an astonishing memory. Both of them are natural narrative theorists, though because of the differences in their capacities for abstraction, I wound up testing their narrative theories in different ways.

When Nick was a toddler, I was in my late twenties, and thoroughly uncertain how to do this "parenting" thing. I learned almost as soon as Nick could talk that he loved my stories; he even gave them numbers, though I never did learn his classification system. One of the stories, I admit, was designed for its perlocutionary effect: when my wife and I were graduate students, we could afford only half-day day care, beginning when Nick was two. So we worked out an arrangement whereby I picked Nick up from day care and took him for the afternoon three days a week, on the grounds that we were both writing our dissertations and needed to divide our time equally but I was a faster writer. I decided that for at least part of those afternoons, little Nick could accompany me to the University of Virginia's Alderman Library as I ran down my sources for what became the third chapter of my dissertation. And I decided that it would be a good idea to tell Nick the Story of the Day My Father Lost Me at the Queens Public Library. The hidden message? *Do not leave my side.*[3]

Nick liked stories with drama: the story of how the hockey-camp bus left without me in 1972; the story of how the camp counselor threw me out of the pool; the story of my first day in first grade, when the teacher corrected me for saying I was six when I was still only five (a situation that got worse in the following years, after that teacher decided to skip me into the second grade because of my reading skills). As you might imagine, sometimes Nick's appetite for stories became wearisome. I read to him every night, and I told him stories about people in my life, and I even made up some stuff. But one day when he was about three and a half, on a long car trip in the Midwest, he asked for story after story. And finally I decided to conduct a little experiment. "All right," I sighed. "I have a new story for you. It goes like this: Red. Yellow. Orange. Blue. Violet. Green. Black. Brown. White—"

"Dad!" Nick interjected, annoyed. "That is not a story."

"No?"

"No! It is just a bunch of colors."

"And a bunch of colors is not a story?"

"No! A story has to have things in it."

"Ah," I replied, phase one of the experiment complete. "A story has to have things in it. You are right. OK. Tree. Cloud. Sunshine. Water . . ."

"No, no, no," Nick insisted, more annoyed. "*Things happen* in a story."

"Fair enough," I acknowledged. "The tree blocked the cloud. The sunshine reflected off the water. The flowers grew . . ."

"Dad!!" Nick interrupted, even more annoyed. "That is not a story either."

"But things happen in it," I pointed out.

"But you are not telling why they happen."

Eureka. *In a story things have to happen for a reason.* We were very close, at this point, to E. M. Forster's famous dictum, "'The king died and then the queen died' is a story. 'The king died, and then the queen died of grief' is a plot" (60). As we will see in the following chapter, however, narratives such as Coetzee's *Life and Times of Michael K* challenge the idea that things happen in stories, as does the opening of Beckett's *Murphy*: "The sun shone, having no alternative, on the nothing new" (1).

I realize there is some pathos in this story about stories: the poor beleaguered toddler, simply wanting to be entertained, subjected instead to the whims of his literary-critic father. But I was curious: how, really, did Nick understand the social contract underwriting "stories"? What did he understand as a violation of that contract, and why? Some years later, when he was seven, he picked up my copy of *The Sound and the Fury*. I invited him to read the first page or two, and that exchange became (in the fullness of time, more than twenty years later) the basis for the opening of chapter 2 of this book. Nick had no trouble at all with any of the sentences he read, and yet, after three or four paragraphs, he turned to me quizzically and asked, "What is going on here?"

"That," I had to admit, "is a very good question."

* * *

Jamie learned his alphabet before he started kindergarten at age six; he learned to read at a first-grade level by the time he was eight. Along the way, he somehow taught himself the American Sign Language alphabet and a few simple ASL words by imitating the pictures he saw in a Sesame Street book devoted to the subject. But even though Jamie had developed a profound love of sharks, barn animals, and the movie *Babe* (just like any number of children his age), he didn't really understand stories *as stories*. He had an amazing recall of individual scenes, particularly scenes that involved pratfalls, and he was able to repeat most of the dialogue from the exchange in which Ferdinand the Duck tells Babe the Pig why he wants Babe to go into Farmer Hoggett's house and steal the Hoggetts' alarm clock from the side of the bed. But he didn't understand how much of the movie's plot is predicated on that scene (the issue is whether animals can avoid being eaten by humans if they demonstrate that they are "indispensable," and Ferdinand has decided that he will crow like a rooster each morning in order to stay alive), nor did he understand what it might mean for a plot to be "predicated on a scene" in the first place. Until he was ten, Jamie enjoyed narratives almost as if they were a series of entertaining vignettes.

Then in 2001, we took him to see *Harry Potter and the Sorcerer's Stone*. We feared that the film might be a bit too much for him to take in, from the opening scenes of Harry the Abject Orphan to the climactic sequence in which Voldemort's baleful spirit speaks from the back of Professor Quirrell's head, with all the plot miscues and misdirections along the way (most of which point to Snape rather than Quirrell as the malevolent force in Harry's world). But we were most pleasantly surprised to find that *he got it*—and not because he himself had glasses just like Harry's, not because he dreamed of going to Hogwarts himself. He roundly dismissed all comparisons between himself and Harry. Rather, he got it because he loved the story, and he loved talking about it for weeks, even after he'd seen the film three or four times. Impressed, I asked him if he'd like to read the book on which the film was based, and he responded with hand-rubbing glee.

Thus began his—and my—adventures with Rowling's plots, and Jamie's fascination with the intricacies of plotting. *Harry Potter and the Chamber of Secrets* posed a challenge to him, because, as we learn during Harry's confrontation with Voldemort's younger self, Tom Riddle, most of the action in the novel is attributable to the fact that Voldemort has placed Harry's schoolmate Ginny Weasley under the "Imperius Curse," thereby forcing her to act as his puppet. The plot of the third installment, *Harry Potter and the Prisoner of Azkaban*, is still more demanding, because its denouement depends on a dizzying series of reversals in which we learn that the wizard suspected of numerous murders (as well as the betrayal of Harry's parents to Voldemort), Sirius Black, is entirely innocent, whereas the pet rat of Harry's close friend Ron Weasley, "Scabbers," is in fact the wizard Peter Pettigrew, who has been hiding out for thirteen years to evade capture for the crimes for which he had framed Black. Number four, *Harry Potter and the Goblet of Fire*, introduces us to the internal machinations of the Ministry of Magic; we learn that there are rival factions within the ministry, and that a senior official's son was one of Voldemort's acolytes. Voldemort reappears in human form at the end of that narrative, thanks to the ministrations of ministry apparatchiks and the fugitive Peter Pettigrew, and thereby sets the stage for *Harry Potter and the Order of the Phoenix*, which is devoted to the beginnings of a renewed civil war within the wizarding world. In the penultimate installment, *Harry Potter and the Half-Blood Prince*, Hogwarts's sage headmaster, Albus Dumbledore, serves as Rowling's narratorial double as he walks Harry through his investigations into Tom Riddle's childhood, Riddle's obsession with genealogical purity, and his eventual transformation into Lord Voldemort.

It was astonishing to me that the vast legions of Rowling's readers now included my intellectually disabled child, a child who wasn't expected to be capable of following a plot more complicated than that of *Chicken Little*. And here's what was *really* stunning: Jamie remembered plot details over thousands of pages even though I read the books to him at night, just before he went to bed, six or seven pages at a time. Narrative has been a memory-enhancing device for some time now, ever since bards made a living by chanting family genealogies and cataloguing the ships that laid siege to Troy. But it took Jamie and me eight years to finish all seven novels of this young-adult Proust sequence, and Jamie retained plot details over all that time. This, I remember thinking, is just *ridiculous*.

As for me, I was charmed by Rowling's insistence that the world of magic is also a world of petty bureaucracy and qualifying exams, a world administered by a school in which brilliant professors are hounded from their jobs merely because they are werewolves, and a world in which students experience the ineffable and the inexplicable while they engage in the routine business of scratching out essays—on parchment, with quills, no less—on the History of Magic and the intricacies of Herbology, Potions, Transfiguration, Charms, and the "soft" elective, Muggle Studies (which presents nonmagical peoples, "Muggles," from the Muggle point of view). Jamie was charmed by all of this, too, even if he didn't understand all the ironies involved in depicting the world of magic as a world like our own, in which witches and wizards are more likely to cite the statutes of the Department of International Magical Cooperation or the proper standards for cauldron thickness than a passage from *The Tempest*. But time after time after time, he bolted upright in bed, exclaiming, "So *that's* why Ginny Weasley was opening the Chamber of Secrets!" and "Wait a minute, Sirius Black is *innocent!*" And every time Jamie had an epiphany about Rowling's plots, I knew that he'd had an epiphany about narrative.

Sirius Black's innocence is no trivial matter. As his story unfolds and as later volumes make increasingly explicit, we learn an Important Life Lesson—namely, that the people in charge are often capricious, clueless, and cruel. Jamie could have been horrified by this, but he wasn't. Instead, he began to ask about things like "innocence" and "justice." So Martha Nussbaum, in *Poetic Justice*, gets at this critical question by way of Charles Dickens, and Jamie Bérubé gets at it by way of J. K. Rowling—so what? One's a prolific novelist who writes tripledeckers packed with plot twists and idiosyncratic characters, and the other is a pop-cultural phenomenon with an enthusiastic American readership and a line of products—*A Christmas Carol* chief among them—that has spawned all manner of spin-offs and tie-ins. Both are seductive tale-tellers, and both have had their snooty detractors.

One aspect of Rowling's work has led Jamie to wonder just what it means to be autonomous, though he doesn't use that word. The

Imperius Curse is bad enough, but when you're faced with dark wizards who falsely claim that they followed Voldemort only because they were under the Imperius spell, you've got a conundrum on your hands. The comic version of this conundrum (Rowling tends to explore justice and autonomy by way of comic subplots as well) is provided by the compulsive overachiever Hermione Granger, who takes it into her head to form the Society for the Promotion of Elfish Welfare (S.P.E.W.) in order to free the house-elves from their lives of ceaseless service to wealthy wizard families. Hermione refuses to acknowledge, however, that the house-elves believe that their lives of ceaseless service are right and just, and that Hermione's attempts to "free" them are a profound insult. The house-elves thereby pose substantial questions: What does it mean to be acting under one's own power? How is one to know when one is not acting in one's best interest? Is "happiness" a sufficient criterion for determining an individual's quality of life (here as in *Brave New World*, with its endless supply of soma), or should something less subjective, like "flourishing," be preferred instead?

A critical index of Jamie's increasing sophistication as a reader was that he became increasingly capable of (and delighted by) making thematic connections that enrich his understanding of his other favorite narratives. In the course of our reading of *Half-Blood Prince*, we came upon an extended flashback/exposition in which the young Professor Dumbledore visits eleven-year-old Tom Riddle in the orphanage in order to inform him that he is a wizard and extend him an invitation to Hogwarts. Jamie gasped at Tom's arrogant reaction to Dumbledore's invitation, and, despite his fatigue, stayed awake for another couple of pages. But before we got to that point, I read the following passage: "The orphans, Harry saw, were all wearing the same kind of grayish tunic. They looked reasonably well-cared for, but there was no denying that this was a grim place in which to grow up" (268). I decided to say a few words about the orphanage, and about Harry's odd, complex moment of sympathy for the friendless boy who grows up to become Voldemort. "Did Harry have a happy childhood when he was growing up?" I asked. Jamie shook his head no. "He had the Dursleys," he said. I pointed out that Harry and Voldemort are similar in that they grow up without parents, and that the kids in the orphanages are there because they have no parents either. I added that Jamie might remember the orphanage in the film *Like Mike*, which was in the "heavy rotation" section of Jamie's DVD collection for a while.

"Or *Free Willy*," Jamie suggested. "Yes, that's right," I said with some surprise. "*Free Willy* is also about a kid who is growing up without parents, and who has foster parents, and he has trouble getting used to his new home."

"Or *Rookie of the Year*," Jamie said. "Not exactly," I replied. "In *Rookie of the Year* Henry has his mother, but his mother's boyfriend is a creep, and we don't know where his father went before he was born."

"*Star Wars* too. There's Luke," Jamie said. "Good one! *Great* example!" I cried. Perfect, in fact. *Star Wars* is like a class reunion of the West's major mythological motifs.

"*Mrs. Doubtfire*," Jamie offered. "Nope, that's about parents who are divorced and live in different houses," I said. "But still, in *Mrs. Doubtfire* the father misses his kids and wants to see them, so he dresses up as a nanny."

"What about *Babe*?" Jamie asked.

"Oh yes, that's a very good example," I told him. "Babe has no parents, and that's why he is so happy when Fly agrees to be like his mother."

"And Rex is like his father," Jamie added. "And Ferdinand the duck is like his brother."

Why, yes, Ferdinand *is* like his brother. This had never occurred to me before. But who knew that Jamie was thinking, all this time, about the family configurations in these movies? And who knew that Jamie knew that so many unhappy families, human and pig, are alike?

Jamie and I have revisited *Babe* many times since: he now understands the plot, and we've talked often about whether it is right and just to eat animals, indispensable or otherwise. Jamie isn't giving up his sausage and bacon, by any means, but he now asks where all his food comes from and how it is made. Thus does the analysis of one narrative produce an endless series of cascading and overlapping narratives. Of course, Jamie is not the first person to remark that many compelling narratives, from Moses to Romulus and Remus to *Great Expectations*, from Harry Potter to Luke Skywalker to Bruce Wayne, involve the stories of abject yet powerful orphans. But I'm simply glad that he's in on the conversation. For our species' long-running obsession with narratives about orphans is, in part, the sign of our inability to stop wondering about our beginnings, and about the narrative problem of how to begin; likewise, as Frank Kermode argued in *The Sense of an Ending*, we tell stories partly because we know we are going to die. So it makes every kind of sense that in reading and rereading the saga of Harry Potter, Jamie has become more articulate about his own origins (as a "baby," a "toddler," and a "kid," matching each of these terms to specific eras, like 1993–1995 for "toddler") and more capable of understanding death—the deaths of characters, of family friends, and of his grandparents. The difference between Jamie's mute bewilderment at the death of his maternal grandfather in 2004 and his somber acceptance of my mother's death in 2013 (when he was emotionally mature enough to visit her in her final days, banter with her, and feed her some "smashed" potatoes) is not simply a function of time; it is also a function of narrative, and of Jamie's understanding of the parameters of narrative.

✳ ✳ ✳

But my children, adept narrative theorists though they be, are not my only inspiration for this book. This project is also informed by years of conversations with colleagues in disability studies, my 2013 seminar on narrative and intellectual disability at the School for Criticism and Theory, and two wholly unexpected encounters that subtly but decisively widened the parameters of this study.

The first encounter happened at the 2011 Modern Language Association convention in Los Angeles, and in retrospect is merely amusing—though at the time it seemed like the stuff of professors' anxiety dreams. I was on a panel titled "Narrative and Intellectual Disability," chaired by Rachel Adams. Since that was the working title of this project as of 2011, I thought it would make sense to try to spell out my ideas for this book, and return to matters I had not taken up since the 2004 MLA conference on disability studies hosted by Emory University. Additionally, I was horribly overdue on my contribution to the *Blackwell Companion to American Literary Studies,* and was hoping that writing the MLA paper would get me jump-started on the article. I titled my paper "Disabled Narrative," and traces of it survive in this book. I was trying to get at the question of how narrative irony works when it involves a character with an intellectual disability, a character who is rendered explicitly as someone who is incapable of understanding the story he or she inhabits. I noted that Steinbeck marks Lennie in this way from *Of Mice and Men*'s opening scene:

> Lennie looked timidly over to him. "George?"
>
> "Yeah, what ya want?"
>
> "Where we goin', George?"
>
> The little man jerked down the brim of his hat and scowled over at Lennie. "So you forgot that awready, did you? I gotta tell you again, do I? Jesus Christ, you're a crazy bastard."

"I forgot," Lennie said softly. "I tried not to forget. Honest to God I did, George." (4)

And just as Lennie does not understand where he is going or why, so too will he not understand what is going to happen to him in the book's final pages; in that sense, his intellectual disability provides the structure for the narrative irony, and the narrative irony defines the novel. Lennie knows not what he does, and we know he knows not what he does. But I mentioned *Of Mice and Men* only in passing, opening instead with Benjy Compson of *The Sound and the Fury* and proceeding to a comparison between Elizabeth Moon's *Speed of Dark* and Mark Haddon's *Curious Incident of the Dog in the Night-Time* (this was one reason I was having trouble framing this argument for a volume on *American* literature), because—as I will show in chapter 3—Haddon provides an ingenious (and quite moving) solution to the problem of writing a novel in the voice of a character who (initially) does not understand the narrative he is in, whereas Moon has to skirt that problem by giving us a second level of narrative focalized through characters who do not have autism and who can explain what is at stake in the unfolding of the narrative told by the character who does have autism.

At the last minute, one of my fellow panelists had to pull out of the convention, and Rachel Adams informed us that Rob Spirko would substitute instead, with a paper titled "The Human Spectrum: Human Fiction and Autism." Rob preceded me on the program— and proceeded to deliver a paper about *The Speed of Dark* and *The Curious Incident of the Dog in the Night-Time*, making many of the points and citing many of the passages I had hoped to highlight in my paper. As I listened to Rob, I toyed with the idea of taking the podium and saying simply, "My paper is what Rob said," but just then, he made an offhand reference to the "*Rashomon*-like" narrative sequence in Philip K. Dick's *Martian Time-Slip*. I snapped to attention: this seemed to me to be something worth discussing. I had not written anything about *Martian Time-Slip* in my paper, but I had recently read it and was still trying to figure out what to make of its extraordinary strangeness. And I was thrilled to be able to discuss it at a conference with Rob Spirko, who has worked on disability and science fiction for some time.

I did wind up delivering most of my original paper; Rob's arguments and mine did not overlap completely. But I threw in some extemporaneous remarks about how the narrative sequences in chapters 10 and 11 of *Martian Time-Slip* are not, in fact, *Rashomon*-like. If they were, they would involve four characters telling the same story from drastically different perspectives, narrating significantly different sequences of events, such that the very idea of "the same story" becomes untenable. But they don't. Instead, as I will show in detail in chapter 2, they open by telling the same story almost word for word, and then proceed into disturbing fantasias that cannot be attributed to any one character, even though each character, the following day, feels the aftereffects of the sequence as a whole. The sequence is not merely "about" the perspective of a character with an intellectual disability; it renders intellectual disability in the form of a disabled textuality that cannot be attributed simply to any one character's mental operations.

And when I realized *that*, thanks to the casual remark of a last-minute-replacement speaker giving a fifteen-minute paper at the MLA convention, I realized that I had a critical piece of my argument, a way of talking about intellectual disability and narrative that did not begin and end with the discussion of whether X character has Y disability. I have often remarked, in the intervening years, that I am writing this book simply as a way of getting more people to read *Martian Time-Slip*. It would be a worthy goal in itself.

As for the second encounter: to say that it was "wholly unexpected," as I have done, is actually an understatement. It was pretty much the last thing in the world I might have imagined. It involved a whimsical decision to join Facebook (after years of steadfast, principled resistance) and, relatedly, to go to the fortieth anniversary reunion of my sixth-grade class (not a happy place for me when I was ten, but I thought that the details of tween angst of 1972 were not worth recalling in 2012). My former classmates, it turns out, have a Facebook page "dedicated to all the members of that class who endured and survived the 6th grade at the hands of the mercurial Mrs. Policastro." Etta Policastro was legendary, not just in the school but in the entire district. She was fierce; she was a martinet; she wore the standard-issue Permanent Hair Bun; and she stopped just this side of corporal punishment. And I was one of her two favorite students.

Within a few days of joining Facebook, I was hailed by Mrs. Policastro's other favorite student, one Phyllis Anderson, née Phyllis Eisenson—someone I had not thought about in almost forty years. It was quite clear who Mrs. P's favorites were: she kept a chart on the wall of all the books we had read (Phyllis led, I was second), and late in the year, after our citywide reading and math scores came back, she *announced to the class* that Phyllis and I had scored at the twelfth-grade reading level. This surely endeared us to our peers, as did Mrs. P's decision to cast me and Phyllis as the leads in the French play. (One of my male classmates resented this arrangement so much that he kept a tally of how many mistakes I made in each rehearsal, and over the months of rehearsals never failed to share this information with me. Another passed a note to Phyllis and signed my name to it. Moloch only knows what it said. Such were the details of tween angst in 1972.) For all that, Phyllis and I never spoke a word to each other, at least not in English. I simply assumed that she had her own circle of friends, and I was astonished to learn, forty years later, that her only friend in the class moved away that year, and that she had made a list of New Year's resolutions for 1972 that included the determination *to ignore the class teasers.*

OK, I thought, so that's what sixth grade was like: you've got two shy, bookish kids who feel ostracized by their peers, who then become the very visible favorites of the teacher everyone fears and despises. That's not merely the basis for a friendship. That's the basis for an entire after-school TV movie. And in the course of striking up a conversation with this person forty years after graduation from PS 32 Queens, I happened to mention Madeleine L'Engle's novel *A Wrinkle in Time*, about which I had just been reading; 2012 was the fiftieth anniversary of the book's publication, and in 1972 at least half of our cohort had read it. Phyllis was of course (or so I imagined) Meg Murry, the very smart girl with the long hair and prominent glasses. This rudimentary identification was complicated a bit by the fact that *I* identified more with Meg—with her sense of isolation, helplessness, and vulnerability above all—than with any male character in the book, and by the fact that I did not stop to think that I might be inadvertently saying to my former classmate, "I remember you—you were the girl with glasses and what's more, everybody thought you were a weirdo." Which is kind of a rude thing to say to someone you've never spoken to, especially after forty years.

But in the course of that brief Facebook conversation, as we caught up on partners and kids and professions (literature professor, clinical psychologist), I mentioned that I was sitting at a table across from Jamie, who had just handed me a list of twenty-five kinds of sharks. To which Phyllis replied, "I am sure you did not know that my brother is autistic." Well, I could have plotzed. Needless to say, I did not know that; I did not know anything about this person, starting with the fact that she had a brother. And a brother with autism, in the 1960s (Andy Eisenson was born in 1957). *Oh my goodness*, I thought at once, *what that must have meant for her mother—to have a child with autism at the precise historical moment when autism was being attributed to "refrigerator mothers." How difficult that must have been.* Followed almost immediately by, *Oh goodness, and then along comes this very smart girl, the younger sister. I can't even begin to imagine the family dynamics, except that no, wait, yes I can.* And the story quickly went still deeper: Sylvia Eisenson, Phyllis's mother, was in fact a psychologist in the New York City school system. She was A.B.D. from the University of Illinois at Urbana-Champaign, of all places, where I taught for twelve years. She knew very well what Bruno Bettelheim was doing with Leo Kanner's refrigerator-mothers theory, and had actually written to Bettelheim to tell him that his work was destructive to loving parents. She received a reply from an underling, telling her to get therapy.

All this I learned in the course of one Facebook chat, which somehow went from "Oh yes, I remember you" to serious familial and emotional matters in the course of a few minutes. Life in the disability community can be like that; I remember a conference at which someone introduced herself as the parent of a child with Down syndrome and we wound up talking about our then-teenaged sons' desires for friends, especially girlfriends, within ten minutes. Because there is so much shared terrain, casual conversations can suddenly turn into serious discussions of special needs trusts and the ethics of getting your child or sibling to sign over his power of attorney. And then, a few days later, after Phyllis had gone back to look at her copy of *A Wrinkle in Time*, she wrote:

just read the first chapter of "Wrinkle", and Meg is described with her glasses and braces and general awkwardness. And I thought—that is at least partly why I liked this book so much—there I am, though without the spunk to duke it out with the kid who said something mean about my brother.

When I read that note I had yet another *Oy, what did I say* moment: *Oh yes, I remember you with your glasses and braces and general awkwardness?* (It turns out the braces came later. I did not remember any braces.) But it was the second sentence that grabbed me. No doubt young Phyllis Eisenson, or anyone with a sibling with an intellectual disability, would read *Wrinkle* with that inflection, with a sense of protectiveness for the more vulnerable family member: wasn't this one of the lessons we learned in Reader-Response Criticism 101?

From one angle it is a rudimentary point, a truism: of course we all bring to every text the welter of experiences, associations, encounters, and intertextual relations we have accumulated over the years. Reader-response criticism made much of this rudimentary point for much of the 1970s, with earnest *Critical Inquiry* forums on whether readers or texts make meaning, whether meaning is determinate or indeterminate, and whether the hypothetical "Eskimo reading" of Faulkner's "Rose for Emily" can be ruled out of court.[4] But from another angle, this exchange seemed (and seems) to me to open onto a principle of considerable breadth, one that has not yet been considered by literary criticism influenced by disability studies. It is the complement to the Rob Spirko-induced insight that disability in literary texts need not be located in, or tied to, a specific character with an identifiable disability; it is the Phyllis Eisenson-induced insight that disability in the relation between text and reader *need not involve any character with disabilities at all.* It can involve *ideas about* disability, and ideas about the stigma associated with disability, regardless of whether any specific character can be pegged with a specific diagnosis. This opens the field of criticism considerably; and I am going to insist that this is a good thing, not least because I am determined to cure disability studies of its habit of diagnosing fictional characters.

To begin with, this insight serves as an essential corrective to Ato Quayson's framing of "aesthetic nervousness" in terms of the encounter between disabled and nondisabled characters. For my sixth-grade classmate (and, I suspect, for many people like her), relations between disabled and nondisabled *people* were at stake in the opening pages of *A Wrinkle in Time*, even though the novel itself contains no characters with intellectual disabilities in a family chock full of geniuses. (And I hope, also, that my remarks on *Wrinkle* will help put to rest—or at least demonstrate the superfluity of—recent speculations that Charles Wallace Murry is himself on the autism spectrum.)[5] My argument throughout this book is that even as disability studies has established itself in the humanities in a way that was unthinkable twenty years ago, it has still limited itself to too narrow a range of options when it comes to literary criticism; and though I am (obviously) being facetious about the idea of "curing" disability studies of anything, I am quite serious about the conviction that disability studies limits itself unnecessarily, as a new branch of criticism and theory, whenever it confines itself to determining the disability status of individual characters. Disability studies need not and should not predicate its existence as a practice of criticism by reading a literary text in one hand and the DSM-5 in the other, even when a text explicitly announces that one or more of its characters is (for example) on the autism spectrum. It is not that a character's condition is irrelevant to how we read him or her; rather, we should avoid the temptation to think that a diagnosis "solves" the text somehow, in the manner of those "psychological" interpretations of yesteryear that explain *Hamlet* by surmising that the prince is, unbeknownst to himself, gay.

I bring up that silly interpretive option for *Hamlet* because, as we will see in the following chapter, the revelation that Albus Dumbledore is gay (an insight vouchsafed to us by no less an authority than the author herself) has helped to obscure the role of intellectual disability in determining the course of young Dumbledore's career: here, the realization that *character X has Y disability* stands in place of the more productive realization that *character X does Y because of Z*. But there is more at stake in the Eisenson-induced insight, I think. In opening the question of the potential relations between disabled and nondisabled characters (and readers' potential relations *to* those relations) so as to include characters who are merely presumed to be intellectually disabled by their fellow characters (such as Coetzee's Michael K and Friday), we come to recognize intellectual disability not only as the expression of somatic/neurological conditions but as a trope, a critical and underacknowledged thread in the social fabric, a device for exploring the phenomenon of human sociality as such. This is not merely a matter of remarking that the idiot and the holy fool offer strategic insight into human hierarchies and the contingency of systems of value, though it is partly that; it is also a matter of gauging how literary works depict systems of sociality in part by including characters who either are or are presumed by their fellow characters to be constitutively incapable of understanding or abiding by the social systems by which their worlds operate. As Margaret Atwood's unnamed narrator/protagonist in *Surfacing* bluntly declares, "Being socially retarded is like being mentally retarded, it arouses in others disgust and pity and the desire to torment and reform" (69). Though there is much more to it than that.

The idea that intellectual disability might provide the grounds for a literary examination of "human sociality as such," when combined with the idea that our species is made up of natural-born storytellers, is what leads me to engage with the recent branch of literary criticism known variously as "evocriticism" or "literary Darwinism." In my conclusion, I will argue (among other things) that this branch of criticism is so aggressively invested in the reinstatement of a normative conception of the human—indeed, an "evolutionarily grounded" normative conception—that it has nothing interesting to say about disability as a form of human variation (and nothing very interesting to say about individual literary texts). But one of the evocritics, Blakey Vermeule, has hit upon a fascinating possibility for literary disability studies—paradoxically, by taking one of the most problematic and undertheorized accounts of intellectual disability (in this case, autism) at face value. I will pursue that possibility briefly here, because it will help set the stage for the chapters to follow.

In her 2010 book, *Why Do We Care about Literary Characters?*, Vermeule starts from a most unpromising place: with Simon Baron-Cohen's theory of autism as "mindblindness," a theory that has been enormously influential among cognitive psychologists but has next to no credibility among many people in the autism community. (As we will see later, it is a theory that informs both Mark Haddon's *Curious Incident of the Dog in the Night-Time* and the first edition of Lisa Zunshine's *Why We Read Fiction*.) The idea is that people with autism are "mindblind"—that is, they are incapable of understanding that other people have minds of their own. The empirical/experimental basis for the theory is astonishingly thin: it is called the "Sally-Anne test," and it involves a scenario in which (a) Sally puts an object under a cup, (b) Sally leaves the room, (c) Anne takes the object or puts it under another cup, and (d) Sally returns to the room. The subject is then asked, *Where will Sally look for the object?*, and if the subject is incapable of understanding that Sally is unaware of what Anne has done, the subject is mindblind. The experiment is problematic on its face, as a diagnostic for autism; but for now, I want to suggest that Vermeule does something very strange with it, and in the course of doing so, renders the concept useful to disability studies.

In a chapter devoted chiefly to satire (and its relevance to cognitive psychology, which I will set to one side), Vermeule introduces the notion of "situational mind blindness." In an obvious sense, this is a severe misprision of Baron-Cohen's theory, since mindblindness is not a state one can occupy situationally, much less adopt at will. To make matters worse, Vermeule's discussion is punctuated by remarks such as "Mind blindness is undoubtedly a tragedy for autistics and their families, although some autistics seem to be gifted with heightened visual capacities" (196) and "People who lack mind-reading capacities somehow give us greater insight into our own capacities to dehumanize other people" (198). The proper response to this, in brief, would be something like "People who attribute mindblindness to others give us greater insight into their capacities to dehumanize other people." Interestingly, Vermeule herself comes close to this formulation when she writes, "Situational mind blindness is a trope of dehumanization, albeit a very complex one: the point of it is to deny other people the perspective of rational agency by turning them into animals, machines, or anything without a mind" (195). Again, I have to leave much to the side here—this time, the supposition that animals do not have minds. And because Vermeule adopts Baron-Cohen's theory wholesale, it does not occur to her to suspect that *the attribution of mindblindness is itself a trope of dehumanization.*

However, the idea that mindblindness might be strategically attributed—not to people with autism, here, but to any object of comedic or satiric ridicule (Vermeule considers the trope to be especially useful for, if not constitutive of, satire)—is an insight that leads us away from the actual (diagnosable) attributes of literary characters and toward an understanding of how tropes of stigma and dehumanization might work even in literary texts in which there are no identifiable characters with disabilities. Even more productively, Vermeule's reading of *What Maisie Knew*, earlier in her book, suggests that mindblindness "is a way of acknowledging the social order by opting out of it" (97); in Maisie's case, this entails encouraging her hideous parents to believe that she is intellectually disabled (she is, in other words, playing dumb) so that she will not have to participate in their destructive forms of gamesmanship. "Becoming stupid is Maisie's revenge, her turn of the screw," Vermeule writes. "She opts out of *la ronde* simply because she refuses to be a tool in someone else's hands" (98).

Now we are getting somewhere. The attribution of mindblindness, on the one hand, and a character's strategic adoption of mindblindness, on the other, open onto complex readings of the social text regardless of whether any individual character can be definitively tagged as a person with an intellectual disability, and (even better) regardless of whether the theory of mindblindness has any utility for the understanding of the autism spectrum. Indeed, both strategic and situational mindblindness can be at work even in texts where the character in question is widely suspected (both by his or her fellow characters and by legions of readers) of having an intellectual disability: witness Coetzee's Michael K imagining that he can opt out of the brutal social order of martial law and omnipresent checkpoints: "If I look very stupid, he thought, perhaps they will let me through" (40). Even for Michael K, with his harelip and his slow mind, the adoption of strategic mindblindness is not simply a question of character attributes. It is a question of characters' relations to social systems, and hence to sociality as such. To return to where this train of thought started, from a Facebook chat with a former grade-school classmate, this is why it does not matter whether Charles Wallace Murry is a child on the autism spectrum. What matters is the web of social relations that constitutes other people's responses to Charles Wallace, and that intensifies to Meg's fierce, protective love of him.

* * *

Part of what I am attempting here can be aligned with Tobin Siebers's project in *Disability Aesthetics* and Joseph N. Straus's work in *Extraordinary Measures*. To wit, I hope to offer rigorous formal textual analyses informed by the past two decades of work in disability studies, and yet to broaden the purview of literary disability studies so that the field is not confined to the representation of human bodies and minds in literary texts. This is a bit tricky (as we will see in the following pages), because in all but the most exceptional cases, literary texts engage with issues surrounding physical and intellectual disability by representing human bodies and minds. What else would we be talking about but bodies and minds, if the subject is disability? And yet disability is also, always already, a social relation, involving beliefs and social practices that structure the apprehension of disability—and of putative human "norms." That is why Siebers can apply the insights of disability studies to architecture, urban studies, and city planning, as when he reads Detroit by way of the legacy of American "ugly laws"; that is why Straus can apply the insights of disability studies to modernist experimental music, in a move that draws heavily on Siebers's insight that modernist experimentalism has everything to do with the exploration of disability and nonnormative modes of being human. (That, in turn, is an insight shared and inspired—in a different register, as Siebers notes—by the Nazi curators who put together the "degenerate art" exhibition of 1937 and who promoted an aggressively idealized visual repertoire for the depiction of the human form.) Admittedly, Straus tends to ground his readings of modernist experimentalism in the individual conditions of composers' bodies, as when he suggests that "the fragmented musical surface of [Stravinsky's] *Requiem Canticles*, with its discrete, isolated textual blocks, may be heard as a metaphorical recreation of physical disintegration, of a body fracturing and losing its organic wholeness" largely because "these late-style characteristics may be related to the increasingly difficult physical circumstances of Stravinsky's old age" (87). But the reading of the work as a "metaphorical recreation" of disability in no way depends on whether its composer was infirm or capable of running marathons; the formalist reading affords us insight into the operation of, and the violation of, human social norms that construct our sense of what is right and proper, what is in just proportion and in good working order.

It may be objected here that Siebers's and Straus's work, in extending disability studies beyond the readings of individual bodies and minds, depends more on ideas about physical disability than on ideas about intellectual disability. This is a point I will readily grant, not only with regard to Siebers and Straus but with regard to the following chapter on motive. There is no reason why the idea of disability as narrative "motive" should be confined to intellectual disability; physical disability is deployed as a motive device in countless narratives. The classic example (in disability studies) is *Moby-Dick*, where Ahab's disfigurement is the motive for his determination to turn the voyage of the *Pequod* into something other than your ordinary profit-generating whaling expedition. But examples abound everywhere, especially in speculative fiction, as when George Saunders's "flaweds" in the novella *Bounty* (including the narrator, who has claws in place of feet) try to avoid capture and removal to the Western United States, where they will be enslaved; or as when the leaders of Earth, in C. S. Friedman's *This Alien Shore*, shut down the portals that enable interstellar travel once they learn that traveling at speeds greater than light induces startling genetic mutations. (There is a savvy narrative wrinkle in *This Alien Shore*, however, insofar as the mutants who do eventually learn how to navigate the "ainniq"—the wormholes in space—are marked as intellectually disabled in ways that suggest that they are on the autism spectrum. Not that their specific diagnosis is important; what matters is their narrative function.)

Nevertheless, I stress intellectual disability here for a number of reasons. The first is the simplest: the formal experiments and textual effects I explore in the second and third chapters, dealing with time and self-awareness, are predicated precisely on fictional forms of intellectual disability. Physical disability seems not to implicate features of mind so readily as intellectual disability; though physical disability may involve trauma and other complex psychological and psychoanalytic processes, it does not entail the kind of metacognitive meditations on cognition that I examine here. Another reason has to do with disability hierarchy, and the unfortunate but persistent fact that intellectual disability is more readily and widely deployed as a device of dehumanization than is physical disability; its ramifications for understanding the social, and understanding the social text woven into the literary text, are therefore all the more illuminating.[6] And the last reason has to do with the hierarchy within disability studies itself, which has been challenged in recent years (chiefly by people working on autism and on mental illness)[7] but which remains very much in effect, whereby physical disability stands in for disability *in toto*. The foundational works in the field, like Rosemarie Garland-Thomson's *Extraordinary Bodies*, were quite explicit about this, and indeed much of the disability rights movement (and the fundamental "social model" distinction between impairment, a matter of bodies, and disability, a matter of social relations and built environments) was launched from the (much-needed) perspective of people with physical disabilities.[8] But the foregrounding of physical disability has proven remarkably resilient even when it is not warranted, as evidenced by (to take one prominent example) the many criticisms of the television series *Glee* that took the show to task for featuring a nondisabled actor playing a wheelchair user, criticisms that largely overlooked the fact that the show also features a young woman with Down syndrome portraying a young woman with Down syndrome.[9] This is not to say that the critiques of the show's use of Kevin McHale, the actor playing Artie in a wheelchair, were not warranted; they were, especially with regard to the episode titled "Wheels," in which Artie (a) remarks that he cannot fake his disability, and (b) takes part in a wheelchair dance to Ike and Tina Turner's version of "Proud Mary" that bears no relation to the choreography actually employed by wheelchair dance companies. And it is not to say that the show's portrayal of Becky Jackson, played by Lauren Potter, is beyond criticism as a representation of a young woman with Down syndrome. It is merely to say that the day is (or should be) long past when work in disability studies can allow physical disability to stand in for disability in general, while leaving intellectual disability unmarked and unremarked.

At the same time, I will leave it to others to decide whether the operative term here should be "developmental disability" or "cognitive disability" (or some other variant) rather than "intellectual disability." I have heard numerous arguments in all directions, as is common in the disability community; I remember when the phrase "person with Down syndrome" was to be preferred to "Down syndrome person," on the grounds that the terminology should be "people first"— until some people decided that "people first" terminology had the unfortunate effect of suggesting that a "person with Down syndrome" has Down syndrome and nothing else. I remember when the word "neuroatypical" was to be preferred to references to "autists," "autistics," or "people with autism"—until some people decided that "neuroatypical" had the unfortunate effect of suggesting that everyone who is not on the autism spectrum is neurotypical (which is palpably not the case). So if some people prefer *developmental* or *cognitive* (or some other variant) to *intellectual* disability, I invite them to use those terms in their own work, in the understanding that no terminological choices are beyond criticism. Likewise, as to "disability": I remember the conference session at which someone criticized my use of the term "cognitive disability," not because he objected to the term "cognitive" but because he objected to the term "disability," which, he insisted, should be replaced by "difference." The title of the conference? "Cognitive Disability and Its Challenge to Moral Philosophy." If a speaker's use of the term "disability" is objectionable at a conference expressly devoted to cognitive disability, then all our words are the wrong ones. We will have to find a new language in which to express our need for a new language.

As for my emphasis on the "fictional" nature of the intellectual disabilities I examine here: I am relying on the ancient—and yet always critical—insight that literary characters are not real people. Even when we are talking about literary characters with disabilities (or to whom disabilities can be or have been attributed), we are still not talking about real people. We are talking about fictional people with fictional disabilities—some of whom are presented, in various novels, in terms of their relation to narrative. The fact that the fictional disabilities under study here are intellectual disabilities just makes them all the more appropriate and provocative for the study of fiction. My methodology is formalist throughout, shuttling between plot and technique, content and form, *fabula* (the raw material of a story, arranged in linear temporal order) and *szujet* (the manner in which a story is told), even while acknowledging that none of those oppositions can be maintained in any pure form.

My last prefatory note, then, has to do with the texts I have chosen for this study. Nothing about this project— not even the endless and unavoidable disputes over disability terminology—has given me more anxiety than this. I have mentioned that the idea for this book first took presentable form in my paper for the MLA conference on disability studies in 2004. That paper was occasioned by a rereading of Maxine Hong Kingston's *Woman Warrior*, a rereading that has mostly survived my re-rereadings of the past decade and more. But I soon found myself overwhelmed with possible examples; the phenomenon I observed at work in *The Woman Warrior* suddenly seemed to appear everywhere, in different guises. And the phenomenon itself became more complex the more I looked at it: where first I saw the deployment of intellectual disability as a motive for storytelling in the text, I soon realized that that deployment also had implications for the text's metafictional relation to itself. The question before me was no longer just a question of women driven mad by forms of patriarchy (important though that be), but also a question of a text's struggle, so to speak, to find its narrative relation to characters who became increasingly unable to understand narrative. This train of thought, wending its way through the following years, led me eventually to *Don Quixote*; and yet by the time I felt prepared to give public presentations on intellectual disability and self-awareness in *Don Quixote*, I was met with the question of whether my reading of the *Quixote* didn't also have potential resonance for readings of Nabokov's *Pale Fire*. (Short answer: yes it does. And that is why *Pale Fire* appears in chapter 3.) My initial forays into disability and speculative fiction produced the same result: if I am arguing that disability is central to films like *Total Recall* and *The X-Men*, what do I think of *This Alien Shore*? Or the role of precogs in the fiction of Philip K. Dick? Or Octavia Butler's monumental *Xenogenesis* trilogy? Or Theodore Sturgeon's very weird and unsettling *More Than Human*?[10]

This book is evidence, I hope, that I took those questions seriously, even when I eventually decided, in the cases of Butler and Sturgeon, to leave the work to others (and there is a growing body of terrific work on Butler and disability). But at a certain point I had to put aside my example anxiety and write. This book, as a result, is not comprehensive; it makes no claim to be *A Rhetoric of Intellectual Disability in Fiction*. It may be better, I have decided, to write a short and sharp book, delineating a few of the most important and engaging uses of intellectual disability in fiction, than to attempt the encyclopedic. If these arguments prove persuasive, perhaps they will generate an endless series of cascading and overlapping readings, some of which will inevitably point to the many oversights and missed opportunities I am unable to prevent or anticipate—and some of which might help to suggest that the phenomena I describe here are not idiosyncratic, not limited to a small handful of texts from among the world's vast stores of narratives, but, as I suggested at the outset, ubiquitous.

CHAPTER ONE

Motive

At a critical moment in the eerie "King's Cross" chapter of *Harry Potter and the Deathly Hallows,* which takes place in a limbo after Voldemort has zapped Harry with the "avada kadavra" killing curse, Albus Dumbledore—who was killed at the end of the previous installment, *Harry Potter and the Half-Blood Prince*—tells Harry about the youthful indiscretion that constituted his early (and long-unacknowledged) fascist phase, when he teamed up with the evil genius Gellert Grindelwald to propose a plan for world domination in which Muggles around the globe would be subject to rule by an elite cabal of wizards (led, of course, by Dumbledore and Grindelwald). "You know what happened," Dumbledore says. "You know. You cannot despise me more than I despise myself." Harry protests, "But I don't despise you—" "Then you should," Dumbledore replies, proceeding to explain why:

> "You know the secret of my sister's ill health, what those Muggles did, what she became. You know how my poor father sought revenge, and paid the price, died in Azkaban. You know how my mother gave up her own life to care for Ariana.

"I resented it, Harry."

Dumbledore stated it baldly, coldly. He was looking now over the top of Harry's head, into the distance.

"I was gifted. I was brilliant. I wanted to escape. I wanted to shine. I wanted glory.

"Do not misunderstand me," he said, and pain crossed the face so that he looked ancient again. "I loved them. I loved my parents, I loved my brother and sister, but I was selfish, Harry, more selfish than you, who are a remarkably selfless person, could possibly imagine.

"So that, when my mother died, and I was left the responsibility of a damaged sister and a wayward brother, I returned to my village in anger and bitterness. Trapped and wasted, I thought! And then, of course, he came. . . ."

Dumbledore looked directly into Harry's eyes again.

"Grindelwald. You cannot imagine how his ideas caught me, Harry, inflamed me. Muggles forced into subservience. We wizards triumphant. Grindelwald and I, the glorious young leaders of the revolution." (715–16)

Dumbledore's youthful crisis comes to a head when his brother, Aberforth, returns and throws cold water on Albus's plan to seek the Deathly Hallows with Grindelwald—"I did not want to hear that I could not set forth to seek Hallows with a fragile and unstable sister in tow"—and precipitates a quarrel between Dumbledore and Grindelwald that ends in his sister Ariana's apparently accidental death. Grindelwald flees, and Albus Dumbledore comes to his senses, realizing that "I was left to bury my sister, and learn to live with my guilt and my terrible grief, the price of my shame" (717).

In October 2007, in a talk at Carnegie Hall a few months after the release of *Deathly Hallows*, J. K. Rowling revealed that Dumbledore is gay. The reaction among Rowling's millions of fans was mostly one of surprise, since there are no textual "clues" to Dumbledore's sexual orientation. Apparently, Dumbledore's attraction to Grindelwald was partly ideological, borne of a burning resentment toward Muggles and a self-aggrandizing sense that a person of his brilliance was being wasted in a small wizard village; but it was also sexual, and his alliance with Grindelwald stemmed partly from his love for Grindelwald. But lost in all the commotion and commentary was something obvious, something hidden in plain sight, something explicitly written into the text: Dumbledore's desire to distinguish himself from his suddenly disreputable family, and most of all from his disabled sister.

Indeed, the first desire cannot be disentangled from the second, because the disabled Ariana is the reason for the decline of the Dumbledore family. At age six, Ariana is assaulted by three Muggle boys when they witness her doing magic. The nature of the assault is not made clear. But as Aberforth explains to Harry and Hermione Granger, "it destroyed her, what they did. She was never right again" (364). She winds up confined to her house for the rest of her life, and the Dumbledore family concocts a cover story—the story of "ill health" Albus mentions to Harry. "She wouldn't use magic," Aberforth explains, "but she couldn't get rid of it; it turned inward and drove her mad, it exploded out of her when she couldn't control it, and at times she was strange and dangerous." Her father "went after the bastards that did it," but does not explain himself to the wizard authorities, "because if the Ministry [of Magic] had known what Ariana had become, she'd have been locked up in St. Mungo's for good" (364). This, then, is why Dumbledore *père* is sent to the remote wizard prison, Azkaban. As for Dumbledore *mère*, she is accidentally killed when Ariana is fourteen and unable to control one of her rages. Albus is therefore compelled to return home upon graduating from Hogwarts, very much against his wishes; but, as Aberforth notes with great bitterness, he wasn't much of a caretaker:

"He was always up in his bedroom when he was home, reading his books and counting his prizes, keeping up with his correspondence with 'the most notable magical names of the day' . . . *he* didn't want to be bothered with her. . . . Bit of a comedown for Mr. Brilliant, there's no prizes for looking after your half-mad sister, stopping her blowing up the house every other day." (365–66)

This, writes the tabloid journalist Rita Skeeter (with more warrant than usual, for her), was "the best-kept secret of Dumbledore's life" (355), not the relatively uncontroversial (and, in the world outside the text, widely welcomed) news that Albus Dumbledore is gay.

What Rowling is doing with the tale of Ariana is more than backstory, more than the standard "as you know, Bob" mode of exposition (though the Harry Potter series includes plenty of that, as well). Rowling is installing intellectual disability at the heart of a narrative that includes no direct representation of a character with intellectual disabilities. We never meet Ariana, not even in flashback; the only representation of her is the portrait on Aberforth's wall, which turns out to be a top-secret magical portal to Hogwarts (all the other secret passages are being watched). Ariana's only "action" in the plot of *Deathly Hallows* is to serve as the spectral vehicle for that spectral portal. But her larger thematic function is decisive, and sets her "brilliant" brother's life on its trajectory: he becomes infatuated with Grindelwald, and the ideal of wizard authoritarianism, partly because he is ashamed of his association with his disabled sister and (justifiably) furious at the Muggles who are the cause of his sister's condition, his father's imprisonment, and (indirectly) his mother's death. Ariana's death, in turn, becomes the impetus for Dumbledore's revaluation of values, his emphatic turn against Grindelwaldism, and his lifelong commitment to Muggle rights, tolerance for all magical creatures, and struggles against entrenched hierarchies and unjustifiable inequalities of all kinds.

Intellectual disability, then, serves as the ethical core of a narrative in which it never explicitly appears. "Ethical core" is Ato Quayson's term, and it is crucial to his groundbreaking concept of "aesthetic nervousness": "disability," Quayson writes, "returns the aesthetic domain to an active ethical core that serves to disrupt the surface of representation" (19). Much of my argument here will elaborate and extend this critical insight, and Quayson's more programmatic statement that "the representation of disability oscillates uneasily between the aesthetic and the ethical domains, in such a way as to force a reading of the aesthetic fields in which the disabled are represented as always having an ethical dimension that cannot be easily subsumed under the aesthetic structure" (19). My readings will try to put pressure on the ideas of "disruption" and "oscillation" at work here; additionally, at times my argument will have less to do with the representation of characters with intellectual disabilities *as* characters than with the question of these characters' relation(s) to narrative—the specific narrative they inhabit, and to narrative as such. (As we will see, depending on the nature of the intellectual disability and the parameters of the narrative in which it occurs, the meaning of "narrative as such" can range from "individual stories" to "entire lives" to "unimaginable time scales.") Finally, following Quayson's suggestion that "the final dimension of aesthetic nervousness is that between the reader and the text" (15), I will turn to a number of literary narratives in which, unlike *Harry Potter* (where Ariana's disability is a motive force in Dumbledore's life and in the narrative he creates for himself), intellectual disability warps the very fabric of the text itself, producing "disabling" effects in readers' comprehension of narrative. This argument will involve narratives in which intellectual disability not only produces what Quayson calls a "hermeneutic impasse" within the text (with regard to content) but also sets the terms for readers' engagement with the text (with regard to form).

But before I get to these readings, I must pause over two aspects of Quayson's argument. The first concerns this "ethical core": whence does it appear? In *Aesthetic Nervousness* it is presented almost as a fact of nature, an uninterrogated lump, itself an ethical core within Quayson's text. The example from *Harry Potter* is straightforward in this respect; after all, Dumbledore *père* winds up in Azkaban for his retaliation against the Muggle boys, so it does not require much digging to find that questions of justice are at stake. For what is the appropriate moral response to a disabling assault on a young child? What are the obligations of her family members to the larger (wizard) society they inhabit? What, in turn, are the obligations of the larger society to the disabled child? It does not appear that wizard society offers much in the way of "reasonable accommodation"; the reason Ariana is kept at home, with lethal consequences for her mother, is that the only alternative is institutionalization in St. Mungo's Hospital for Magical Maladies and Injuries. The question of justice confronts us at every turn, and surely the ethical core proceeds from or is structured by that question in its various forms. And as we will see in the following chapters, there is an ethics of narrative at stake as well, and the animating question will be what the character with an intellectual disability knows—or can know—about the narrative she or he inhabits.

But the ethical core need not be triggered by the presence of, or even by a reference to, a character with an intellectual disability. Intellectual disability can be a textual matter—a matter for the text, and a motive for its characters—even when there are no characters with intellectual disabilities to be found. As I suggested in the introduction, this is what is at stake in *A Wrinkle in Time*. Fourteen-year-old Meg Murry has been dropped to the lowest section in her grade—one of her frustrated teachers says, "I don't understand how a child with parents as brilliant as yours are supposed to be can be such a poor student" (11)—partly because she is a discipline problem. Her peers consider her to be a dim-witted troublemaker. And one of the reasons for Meg's bad behavior is that everyone believes that she has an intellectually disabled sibling:

> On the way home from school, walking up the road with her arms full of books, one of the boys had said something about her "dumb baby brother." At this she'd thrown the books on the side of the road and tackled him with every ounce of strength she had, and arrived home with her blouse torn and a big bruise under one eye. (12)

L'Engle's readers know that Meg's five-year-old brother, Charles Wallace, is not dumb. Though he is a late-talking child, he is (as he himself knows) a biological sport, a mutation, an anomalously brilliant child who has a grasp of general relativity and possesses some telepathic powers on the side even though he does not yet know how to read. Indeed, he is savvy enough to know that it is probably best if people do not think much of him: "I'm afraid it will make it awfully hard for me in school next year if I already know things. I think it will be better if people go on thinking I'm not very bright. They won't hate me quite so much" (34).

Both Murry parents have multiple doctorates in the sciences (the father is a physicist, the mother a microbiologist); the family is practically bursting with big brains. But the *stigma* of intellectual disability haunts Meg and Charles Wallace, whom people think of as "morons"—or, more politely, as being a few cards short of a full deck, especially when compared to the unremarkable ten-year-old twins, Sandy and Dennis: "The two boys seem to be nice, regular children, but that unattractive girl and the baby boy certainly aren't all there"

(16). Here, the stigma associated with intellectual disability structures the Murry household, precisely *because* the Murry household is so defined by and invested in intelligence, with Meg seeking to avoid or contest the stigma (hence the fisticuffs upon hearing a random unkind word) and Charles Wallace seeking to find a shelter in stigma in order to avoid becoming the object of fear and hatred: better to be thought a moron than a freak. The ethical core at the heart of *A Wrinkle in Time*, then, does not arise from any one character or any one set of attributes, but from the more generalized presence of social stigma.

I want to establish this point early in my argument because (a) it is counterintuitive—who thinks of *A Wrinkle in Time* in terms of disability?—and (b) it gets at one of the key limitations of Quayson's otherwise capacious framework, his insistence that "the primary level" of aesthetic nervousness "is in the interaction between a disabled and nondisabled character, where a variety of tensions may be identified" (15). It is notable that Quayson characterizes that interaction in terms of "nervousness"; the term suggests a potentially productive anxiety and unease, and is therefore more supple—and even more hopeful—than terms like "disgust," "repulsion," or "horror" (reactions that are far from unthinkable, and in many times and places were the normate norm). No doubt the concept owes much to Erving Goffman's staging of that encounter: "When normals and stigmatized do in fact enter one another's immediate presence . . . there occurs one of the primal scenes of sociology" (13). What is most appealing about Quayson's formulation, in other words, is that it has the potential to reframe that primal scene, recasting the disgust, repulsion, or horror evinced by nondisabled characters in the presence of disability as a matter of *aesthetic* nervousness. One thinks of the visceral disgust with which Victor Frankenstein first beholds his creature, and then one thinks, with Quayson, of how that encounter "is augmented by tensions refracted across other levels of the text such as the disposition of symbols and motifs, the overall narrative or dramatic perspective, the constitution and reversals of plot structure, and so on" (15). "Aesthetic nervousness" allows even the most horrified (and horrifying) encounters with disability to be transformed into something else, something potentially revelatory, something that raises questions not only with regard to the ethical core of a text but also with regard to its form and texture.[1] And yet the theory remains based on the representation of characters with disabilities, rather than on textual tropes, rhetorical devices, and narrative strategies for constructing (and deconstructing) disability.

Likewise, David Mitchell and Sharon Snyder's theory of "narrative prosthesis" is more a theory about characters with disabilities than a theory about narrative. But because "narrative prosthesis" is the single most influential account of narrative in disability studies, I should explain the differences between Mitchell and Snyder's work and the kind of inquiry I am pursuing here. Published in 2000, *Narrative Prosthesis: Disability and the Dependencies of Discourse* is a landmark work, a field-defining theoretical statement that any subsequent account of disability and narrative cannot fail to address (and, indeed, Quayson's theory of "aesthetic nervousness" does address it, and there are many points of overlap between the two books). Very much like Quayson, Mitchell and Snyder insist that "within literary narratives, disability serves as an interruptive force that confronts cultural truisms" (48), but their account of that interruptive force relies cannily on the claim that disability is always the occasion for interpretation; it always signifies something other than itself, it is always rendered as enigma and challenge:

> It is the narrative of disability's very unknowability that consolidates the need to tell a story about it. Thus, in stories about characters with disabilities, an underlying issue is always whether their disability is the

foundation of character itself. The question is not whether disability is cause or symptom of, or distraction from, a disturbing behavioral trait, but whether its mystery can be pierced by the storyteller. (6)

In some cases, however, the representation of disability is not mysterious at all; when Mitchell and Snyder write that "disability pervades literary narrative, first, as a stock feature of characterization and, second, as an opportunistic metaphorical device" (47), one thinks of a text like Richard Wright's *Native Son*, which renders disability metaphorical in such a way as to suggest that sightless eyes are a window on the soul, as in the unsavory moment in Boris Max's defense of Bigger Thomas at which he turns to the woman whose daughter Bigger has killed, crying, "And to Mrs. Dalton, I say: 'Your philanthropy was as tragically blind as your sightless eyes!'" (393). I call the moment "unsavory" because it cannot possibly be a wise defense strategy to blame Mrs. Dalton for the death of her only child, and because Max does so in a narrative that has already made remarkably heavy-handed use of the trope of blindness, as when Bigger thinks, "Jan was blind. Mary had been blind. Mr. Dalton was blind. And Mrs. Dalton was blind; yes, blind in more ways than one" (107).

Native Son deploys disability so as to render disability as a moral failing, and manages, in so doing, to ignore the material detail of the disability itself: it may be crucial to the plot that Mrs. Dalton was not able to see Bigger in Mary's room that night, but once Mrs. Dalton has performed her function in the plot, her blindness is important to *Native Son* only in a metaphorical sense. This, surely, is what Mitchell and Snyder mean by an "opportunistic" metaphorical device. But Mitchell and Snyder's theory of narrative prosthesis goes well beyond this, opening onto strategies for reading that are inventive and provocative—and yet, as we shall see, potentially reductive as well. Mitchell and Snyder start from the salutary point that disability is

often underrecognized by readers, even though "disability has func-
tioned throughout history as one of the most marked and remarked
upon differences that originates the act of storytelling" (54). This is
a version of the above claim that disability demands a story; for an
illustration of this principle I usually turn to my sister-in-law's business partner, one of whose arms ends at the elbow. Over the years,
she has grown weary of people asking her what happened to her arm;
noting that the people who were rude enough to ask tended also to
be people who were visibly (if subtly) disappointed in the answer that
she was born this way, she began to reply, with an affect somewhere
between deadpan and insouciant, "shark attack." For Mitchell and
Snyder, however, stories that are inaugurated by disability follow a
post-shark-attack trajectory that forms one aspect of their theory of
narrative prosthesis, inasmuch as the narrative works to make the
disability disappear:

> A simple schematic of narrative structure might run thus: first, a devi-
> ance or marked difference is exposed to a reader; second, a narrative
> consolidates the need for its own existence by calling for an explana-
> tion of the deviation's origins and formative consequences; third, the
> deviance is brought from the periphery of concerns to the center of
> the story to come; and fourth, the remainder of the story rehabilitates
> or fixes the deviance in some manner. (53)

This simple schematic holds up very well for certain Disney animated
films as well as mainstream Hollywood fare like the 1997 James L.
Brooks film *As Good as It Gets*.[2] The preferred mode of Disneyfication
involves resignifying a character's disability as a unique and valuable
talent, as when Dumbo's ginormous ears turn out to be the species
anomaly that enables him to fly (and to become the circus's central
attraction). Relatedly, a character's disability can be compensated for

by a unique and valuable talent, as in *Happy Feet*, when Mumble, a penguin who is unable to sing a "heartsong" to attract a mate and who is ostracized by his fellow penguins as a result (and whose disability may have something to do with the fact that his father did not take proper care of the egg during incubation), turns out to be a species-anomalous tap-dancing penguin whose talent eventually helps save his species.[3]

However, it is not clear that this narrative structure will hold for all, or even most, depictions of disability in narrative (it will not work for Ariana Dumbledore in *Harry Potter*), let alone fictions like *A Wrinkle in Time* where the stigma of intellectual disability operates even in the absence of any characters with intellectual disabilities. And even when narratives do work to efface disability, to rehabilitate or fix the deviance that provides the story with its central motive, the theory of narrative prosthesis as advanced by Mitchell and Snyder seems to run in two different directions. The first direction leads to the conclusion that narrative about disability is not merely opportunistic but parasitic: "Our phrase *narrative prosthesis* is meant to indicate that disability has been used throughout history as a crutch upon which literary narratives lean for their representational power, disruptive potentiality, and analytical insight" (49). Leaving aside the obvious objection that literary narratives have at their disposal a wide array of devices for generating representational power, disruptive potentiality, and analytical insight, the most important aspect of this claim is that narrative thereby does a disservice to actual people with disabilities, insofar as "while stories rely upon the potency of disability as a symbolic figure, they rarely take up disability as an experience of social or political dimensions" (48). A more disturbing corollary of this claim holds that "disability inaugurates narrative, but narrative *inevitably* punishes its own prurient interests by overseeing the extermination of the object of its fascination" (56–57; emphasis mine), and that corollary follows from the insistence that "*all* narratives operate out of a desire to compensate for a limitation or to reign [*sic*] in excess" (53; emphasis mine). I will get back to these matters of inevitability and inexorability in a moment, but for now, it should suffice to suggest that this aspect of narrative prosthesis offers a disability-studies version of the hermeneutics of suspicion, in which narrative engages with disability to nefarious, "prurient," and potentially harmful ends. As Mitchell and Snyder write in their opening pages,

> Beyond this elucidation of disability as transgressive of social ideals, this literary strategy also has a visceral effect on the lives of disabled people. While disability's troubling presence provides literary works with the potency of an unsettling cultural commentary, disabled people have been historically refused a parallel power within their social institutions. In other words, while literature often relies on disability's transgressive potential, disabled people have been sequestered, excluded, exploited, and obliterated on the very basis of which their literary representation so often rests. Literature serves up disability as a repressed deviation from cultural imperatives of normativity, while disabled populations suffer the consequences of representational association with deviance and recalcitrant corporeal difference. (8)

It is no wonder, then, that Mitchell and Snyder are tempted—though they finally (and wisely) refuse the temptation—to "condemn the literary as bankrupt with regard to disability" (9).

The other direction, however, leads not to the conclusion that narrative inevitably effaces or exterminates disability (and contributes to the immiseration of people with disabilities), but rather that the effort to efface or exterminate disability in some literary texts often fails, and in its failure, offers a disability-studies version of the Russian formalist belief, first enunciated by Viktor Shklovsky, that the function of the literary is to "lay bare the device." Here, Mitchell and Snyder start by asserting the reparative function of the prosthesis, but turn instead to the argument that the device ultimately serves to lay itself bare:

> While an actual prosthesis is always somewhat discomforting, a textual prosthesis alleviates discomfort by removing the unsightly from view. . . . [T]he erasure of disability via a "quick fix" of an impaired physicality or intellect removes an audience's need for concern or continuing vigilance. . . . The prosthetic function in most of the works that follow, then, is to undo the quick repair of disability in mainstream representations and beliefs. In part, this book is about the literary *accomplishment* of a faulty, or at least imperfect, prosthetic function. *The effort is to make the prosthesis show, to flaunt its imperfect supplementation as an illusion.* The prosthetic relation of body to word is exposed as an artificial contrivance. Disability services an unsettling objective in these literary works by refusing its desired cultural return to the land of the normative. Ironically, the accomplishment of the works under scrutiny here is to expose, rather than conceal, the prosthetic relation. (8; emphasis in original)

I suspect that the word "ironically" is the key to this line of thinking: the prosthesis tries to hide the unsightly from view, as in the argument that narrative serves to rehabilitate or fix deviance, but despite itself, winds up calling attention to itself, thereby exposing rather than concealing the prosthetic relation.

In this schema, the undecidability of disability is most likely related to the phenomenon whereby disability is presented as riddle and enigma, a mystery to be pierced by the storyteller. This aspect of Mitchell and Snyder's theory has startling implications for the practice of literary criticism, implications that I think have largely gone unremarked to date. Their skepticism about interpretation stems from a well-grounded sense that some bodies are more legible, more marked, than others:

> The problem of the representation of disability is not the search for a more "positive" story of disability, as it has often been formulated in disability studies, *but rather a thoroughgoing challenge to the undergirding authorization to interpret that disability invites.* There is a politics at stake in the fact that disability inaugurates an explanatory need that the unmarked body eludes by virtue of its physical anonymity. (59–60)

Here, one is left with the impression that the disabled body is always already matter for interpretation *and the nondisabled body is not.* That impression is strengthened at the end of Mitchell and Snyder's chapter "Narrative Prosthesis and the Materiality of Metaphor," where they write, "If the nondysfunctional body proves too uninteresting to narrate, the disabled body becomes a paramount device of characterization" (64). That is an enormous "if," asking us to agree that narratives tend to avoid telling the stories of nondysfunctional bodies because those stories are not sufficiently interesting. But even more important, one is left with the impression that interpretation itself does violence to disability—and people with disabilities:

> The knee-jerk impulse to interpretation that disability has historically instigated hyperbolically determines its symbolic utility. This subsequent overdetermination of disability's meanings turns disabled populations into the vehicle of an insatiable cultural fascination. Literature has dipped into the well of disability's meaning-laden depths throughout the development of the print record. In doing so, literary narratives bolstered the cultural desire to pursue disability's bottom-

less interpretive possibilities. The inexhaustibility of this pursuit has led to the reification of disabled people as fathomless mysteries who simultaneously provoke and elude cultural capture. (61)

There is, of course, much in the historical record to justify this skepticism about the hermeneutic enterprise with regard to disability. Not only has disability been taken as a sign of God's wrath or God's grace in a variety of religious traditions (bespeaking divine punishment or divine election), but as the administration of disability passed from the religious order to the medical over the course of the past two centuries, the disabled body became the object of biopower, defined by the medical and medicalizing gaze that could determine whether a body was to be institutionalized, sterilized, or (quite often, in the history of the United States) shipped back from Ellis Island to its country of origin. Rarely is the interpretation of disability in the social sphere benign, let alone beneficial, to the people being interpreted. But I want to stress how counterintuitive this injunction against interpretation should be for literary criticism. It is as if disability should not mean but be, as if depictions of disability should involve (say) blindness, deafness, schizophrenia, or achondroplasia with no other semiotic functions or implications.

There are, however, literary texts and traditions in which disability is presented simply as disability, and not as a sign of something other than itself. In an unpublished paper titled "When the Saints Come Crippin' In," Alice Sheppard argues that whereas Christian writers of the first millennium typically understood disability as a sign of one's moral state or as an occasion for charity and/or miraculous cure, Old Norse epics present disability simply as itself—as a war wound with no greater semiotic significance, or as cleft lip and palate signifying nothing other than cleft lip and palate. A more contemporary example can be found in *Moby-Dick*, which may be of more interest to disability studies insofar as Captain Ahab, like Shakespeare's Richard III, is often adduced as an example of a character deformed by disability: as Mitchell and Snyder argue, Ahab is led to megalomania and madness by the loss of his leg to the white whale. But as James Berger has pointed out in response to Mitchell and Snyder, Melville's text contains a countervailing example, that of Captain Boomer of the *Samuel Enderby*, who has lost an arm to Moby-Dick and tells Ahab emphatically (and cheerfully) that he wants nothing more to do with the whale: "He's welcome to the arm he has, since I can't help it, and didn't know him then; but not to another one. No more White Whales for me; I've lowered for him once, and that has satisfied me" (340). For Captain Boomer, then (and, at least in this instance, for Melville), a lost arm is nothing more than a lost arm. Thus, writes Berger, "I agree with [the] description of Ahab as semantic terrorist, but am not convinced by Mitchell and Snyder's argument that his status is entirely a function of his disability" (170). Sometimes, it appears, the representation of disability involves no metarepresentation of the thing(s) the disability itself is understood to represent. The disabled cigar is just a disabled cigar.

This uncontroversial observation has profound implications for the theory of narrative prosthesis, leading me to want to qualify Mitchell and Snyder's most sweeping claims about what all narratives inevitably do. But Berger's argument has profound implications for my own work as well, which I should address at once. The argument that disability does not work toward one determined end, or follow one inescapable trajectory, in *Moby-Dick* (or, for that matter, in any literary text) is central to this book, even if it imposes severe limits on the range and scope of my analyses. That is, I am committed here not to the project of encyclopedic typology but to the affirmation of radical individuation. It is a truism in the intellectual disability community that when you have met one person with autism, you have met . . . exactly one person with autism. The range of behaviors and possible positions on the autism spectrum are simply too bewilderingly diverse to admit of generalization.[4] The same is true, to an extent, with the condition I know best, Down syndrome; though the underlying biochemistry, the chromosomal nondisjunction and its genetic consequences, may be the same (hence the "syndrome" part of Down syndrome), the expression of trisomy-21 throughout the human population spans a wide range of talents, deficits, and proclivities. I am going to insist, therefore, on a radically Heraclitean understanding of disability and narrative, whereby we can never step in the same interpretive river twice. And I want to up the ante on the truism about autism: when you've met one person with autism, you've met one person with autism . . . *once.* The next time you meet that person, he or she will be slightly different, and so will you. The same holds true for literary characters: when you meet one Captain Ahab, or Michael K, you have met one Captain Ahab, or Michael K, *once.* The next time you encounter them, they too will be slightly different, and so will you.

The relation between the literary and the nonliterary (or what is called, by some holdouts in remote outlying precincts of the profession, the real world) is critical to the most important point of intersection between Mitchell and Snyder's theory of narrative prosthesis and Quayson's theory of aesthetic nervousness. In a passage that seems to run athwart the claim that disability invites an "undergirding authorization to interpret," Mitchell and Snyder write that the presence of disability in a text produces a glitch in the hermeneutic machinery: "Disability recurs . . . as a potent force that challenges cultural ideals of the 'normal' or 'whole' body. *At the same time, disability also operates as the textual obstacle that causes the literary operation of open-endedness to close down or stumble*" (50; emphasis in original). Quayson acknowledges that this aspect of Mitchell and Snyder's work "brings their discussion of narrative prosthesis very close to my own notion of aesthetic nervousness," but takes his distance from it on the grounds that "they proceed to expound upon this blocking function in what can only be nonaesthetic terms" (25). "This is how they put it," he writes:

> This "closing down" of an otherwise permeable and dynamic narrative form demonstrates the historical conundrum of disability. [Various disabled characters from literature] provide valuable counterpoints to their respective cultures' normalizing Truths about the construction of deviance in particular, and the fixity of knowledge systems in general. Yet each of these characterizations also evidences that the artifice of disability binds disabled characters to a programmatic (even deterministic) identity. (Mitchell and Snyder 2000, 50)
>
> Thus Mitchell and Snyder's idea of the shutting down or stumbling of the literary operation is extrinsic to the literary field itself and is to be determined by setting the literary representations of disability against the socio-cultural understandings. . . . Also, I would like to disagree with them on their view of the programmatic identity assigned to the disabled, because, as I will try to show by reading the disabled character within the wider discursive structure of relations among different levels of the text, we find that even if programmatic roles were originally assigned, these roles can shift quite suddenly, thus leading to the "stumbling" they speak of. I choose to elaborate the textual "stumbling" in terms of aesthetic nervousness. (25)

This polite disagreement, and the invocation of the extrinsic that precedes it, opens onto questions of enormous scope. What is the nature of "the literary operation of open-endedness," and how can it be made to close down or stumble? Perhaps the encounter with a character like

Ahab, whose quest is not only for the White Whale but for a system of fixed, stable meanings, provides an answer: disability disrupts any regime of signification into which it enters. We are very close here to Quayson's notion of an active ethical core in the depiction of disability that serves to disrupt the surface of representation. But is it illegitimate to appeal to the extraliterary for justifications concerning representation? What are literary representations representations *of*, if not of the extraliterary? And who in disability studies—who in any realm of endeavor—would want to pursue an inquiry into the representation of disability in literature that did *not* have implications and possible consequences for the lives of people with disabilities? One strains to imagine a branch of queer theory that proceeds as an academically sanctioned interpretive enterprise but has no concern for the lives and livelihoods of queer people. What would be the point of the enterprise if it were "academic" in the sense of an "academic" question, a moot point, a question that does not matter?

And yet one does not want to make the case for the study of disability in literary criticism (if "one" is me) solely on the grounds that it is important for reasons that derive from social policy rather than from protocols of reading. There must be something about the reading of disability *as reading* that changes the way we read, just as there was something about queer theory *as a theory of reading* that secured queer theory's role in the contemporary canon of literary criticism and theory. When Carol Poore writes that the critique of representations of disability "is necessary because of the grave consequences these widely accepted negative images had and still have for the lives of people with disabilities" (261), I want to say that the object is unimpeachable—but that it does not tell us why that critique should be part of the apparatus of literary criticism (as opposed to media studies, communication, sociology, or policy studies). What does the study of disability tell us about the practices of reading?

Even though Mitchell and Snyder predicate one aspect of their theory—on the stumbling or shutting-down of the open-endedness of
the literary text—on what Quayson rightly calls extraliterary criteria,
they, like Quayson, are clearly making claims about what the study
of disability in literature brings to the discipline of literary criticism
(and particularly to the study of narrative). The limitation of their
account is that it has more or less the degree of programmatic deter-
minism they ascribe to narrative prosthesis, whereby narrative always
and inevitably does X. My contention is more modest, but more de-
fensible: some narratives do X. Some do not.

In contrast to Mitchell and Snyder, Quayson offers a more varied
and supple reading of disability and narrative insofar as his "typology of disability representation" enumerates no fewer than nine possible functions for aesthetic nervousness: disability as null set and/or
moral test (as in *A Christmas Carol*, *The Sound and the Fury*, or the
film *There's Something about Mary*); disability as the interface with
otherness (race, class, sexuality, and social identity); disability as ar-
ticulation of disjuncture between thematic and narrative vectors (as
in Disney's *Finding Nemo*); disability as moral deficit/evil; disability
as epiphany (as in *To Kill a Mockingbird*); disability as signifier of
ritual insight (as in the case of Tiresias); disability as inarticulable
and enigmatic tragic insight (as in *One Hundred Years of Solitude*);
disability as hermeneutical impasse (as in *The English Patient*, and, as
we shall see, in Coetzee's *Foe* and *Life and Times of Michael K*); and
disability as normality.[5]

The category of disability as normality is of particular interest to
me, and not merely because Quayson assigns my own book, *Life as
We Know It*, to that category.[6] For Quayson, aesthetic nervousness
denotes the process by which "the dominant protocols of representation within the literary text are short-circuited in relation to disability" (15). The category of disability as normality, however, seems to be

exempt from the dynamics of aesthetic nervousness—and it seems to be dominated by nonfiction, memoirs, and autobiographies. Discussing *Life as We Know It* and Robert Murphy's book *The Body Silent*, Quayson writes,

> In both of these instances, the accounts are being written with a full sense of the complexity of responses that attend disability; it is not a stereotype or condition that can be easily assimilated to an essentialized category. Thus, even though there is often some degree of nervousness and anxiety about the implications of living with a disability, there is none of the aesthetic nervousness that we find in the literary accounts. . . . Since in the (auto)biographies of persons with disability the representation is conducted consistently from the point of view of the persons with disabilities and their caregivers, the opportunities for a "collapse" of the dominant protocols are curtailed. (51)

The category thus roughly corresponds to Rosemarie Garland-Thomson's "realistic" mode of visual representation, in which disability is simply itself, and not (in Garland-Thomson's typology) wondrous, sentimental, or exotic.[7] But it is problematic for the same reason that Garland-Thomson's category is problematic: "the real" is not a self-explanatory realm where things are just what they are. In literature and the visual arts, "realism" is an effect of protocols of representation, devices and techniques that produce the illusion of mimesis; "the real" is what appears when a master artificer has deployed those devices with an art that conceals the art. It is no wonder that Quayson is drawn to nonfiction for this category, and yet nonfiction, like fiction, is made up of language, the same slippery stuff that opens onto deconstructive rabbit holes in the work of Melville or Montaigne. "Realism" cannot stand as an uninterrogated category after Roland Barthes has finished rereading and rewriting

Balzac's "Sarrasine" in *S/Z*; nor can it escape the warping effects of queerness once one comes to terms with the fact that one of the categories in the drag balls documented in *Paris Is Burning* is that of "realness."[8]

For my purposes, then, the "real" and the "normal" should (and will) be considered just as weird as everything else we humans do when we represent people and events to each other in the form of narratives. I do not deny that there are texts, like the one I wrote in my attempt to represent my son at a young age, that try to render disability as ordinary rather than extraordinary. But I insist that the strategies for doing so are as artificial as any other strategies employed by artificers—and, more broadly, that the standards for apprehending a text or a visual representation as "artificial" or "realistic" vary considerably by time and place. One of the more ambitious undertakings of this book is to use the study of intellectual disability in narrative to ask what the "real" and the "normal" consist of, and to lay bare the crafty procedures that go into the cultural production of artifacts we now take to be ordinary, straightforward, unproblematic representations of the world.

One final theoretical point before I turn back to readings of literary texts. In the course of *Aesthetic Nervousness*, Quayson never quite explains what "short-circuited" means in the proposition that "the dominant protocols of representation within the literary text are short-circuited in relation to disability." It is possible to read the suggestion casually, whereby "short-circuited" means something akin to "skewed" or just "messed with": disability will derange your dominant protocols of representation. The casual reading has much to recommend it, because there are any number of instances in which disability *will* derange your dominant protocols of representation, as this book will show; yet a short circuit is not the same thing as a derangement (or a skewing, or a messing-with), and the term deserves at least as much scrutiny as the multivalent term "prosthesis" in Mitchell and Snyder. It remains to us, in other words, to do more with Quayson's metaphor than he does. For when electrical current is diverted through an area of lower resistance, some functions that the current is supposed to serve may very well be "disabled," in the sense one uses when one disables a smoke alarm.[9] This residual sense of "disability" carries none of the stigma associated with forms of cognitive or physical disability.[10] No one stigmatizes a smoke alarm by removing its batteries, just as no one denigrates or devalues a function on one's computer by disabling it. "Disabling" an aspect of narrative by way of a short circuit, therefore, implies no normative judgments about what a narrative ought to be.

This may seem to be a banal point. Who would think that the term "disability" is necessarily stigmatizing, or that referring to the disabling of some aspects of narrative necessarily entails a normative view of narrative (or anything else)? The reason for my caution has to do with the general reluctance, in disability studies as in the disability rights movement, to talk about disability in terms of function. Inevitably, it seems, any discussion of functionality with regard to disability will involve some normative ideas about how bodies and minds *should* function (eyes should see, ears should hear, legs should walk, brains should be able to decode facial expressions and distinguish reality from fantasy), and thus any admission that disability involves a reduction or loss of function threatens not only to return us to the idea of disability as lack, but to give up on the foundational distinction between disability (as a social phenomenon) and impairment (as a somatic phenomenon). All disability thereby becomes impairment, and the idea that disability studies examines disability as *the social organization and administration of impairment* is lost altogether. This seems too steep a price to pay for a rigorous reading of Quayson's short circuit.

But there is a way to talk about function without repudiating the key insight into the social character of disability. As John Searle argues in *The Construction of Social Reality*, the dividing line between the world of "brute fact" (rocks, quarks, planets, electromagnetic radiation) and "social fact" (money, institutions, values, forms of government) is provided precisely by the attribution of function. "Functions are never intrinsic to the physics of any phenomenon," Searle writes, "but are assigned from outside by conscious observers and users. *Functions, in short, are never intrinsic but are always observer relative*" (14; emphasis in original).[11] Thus, if one were to say "the heart pumps blood" (this is Searle's example), one would be speaking of brute fact; but if one were to say "the function of the heart is to pump blood," one is in the realm of social fact, because "we are doing something more than recording these intrinsic facts. We are situating these facts relative to a system of values that we hold" (14). So, for example, when Maria Truchman-Tataryn writes, in "Textual Abuse: Faulkner's Benjy," that "interpretations of Benjy perpetuate oppressive stereotypes of disability as diminished in function and therefore in human worth" (515), two points need to be made in response. One is that nothing is gained by denying that some disabilities do entail diminishments in function. The other is that everything is to be gained by disarticulating "degree of function" from "degree of human worth." The point is not to try to pretend that all disabilities are purely a matter of social stigma; the point, rather, is to insist that "function" can never be a meaningful measure of human worth.

Accordingly, I do not see any great peril to the project of disability studies in using Quayson's work to interrogate the functions of narrative. On the contrary, acknowledging that certain narratives are not functioning in the way readers expect them to offers two advantages: first, in pursuing Quayson's suggestion that the final dimension of aesthetic nervousness is that between the reader and the text, we can more adequately account for the readerly experience of trying to navigate texts whose formal experiments are predicated on intellectual disability, such as *The Sound and the Fury, Martian Time-Slip, Pale Fire,* or Chris Nolan's 2000 film *Memento.* Those texts are difficult, as I will explain in more detail, precisely because some features of narrative have been disabled, such that the text prevents, defers, or eludes readerly comprehension—though I will not go so far as to say that these texts disable readers. Second, we can get at the question of how readers expect texts to behave, reanimating one of the central questions of reader-response criticism by way of disability studies and challenging the aggressively normalizing understanding of narrative (and of humans) represented by evocriticism/literary Darwinism. For now, I direct your attention to two literary texts—one clearly fictional, one impossible to classify.

*   *   *

The Woman Warrior is impossible to classify insofar as it is neither fiction nor nonfiction, but, rather, a curious hybrid of memoir, folktale, immigrant narrative, and the supernatural, where ghosts are common, rabbits sacrifice themselves, and there are two people made of gold turning the Earth on its axis. Over the decades since its publication in 1976, it has generally been understood both as a landmark in Asian American literature and as a feminist critique of women's silencing under patriarchy, opening dazzlingly with a fearsome injunction to silence and its transgression: "'You must not tell anyone,' my mother said, 'what I am about to tell you'" (3). There is no question that *The Woman Warrior* is a landmark in Asian American literature and a feminist critique of women's silencing under patriarchy. What is astonishing, however—and sadly underremarked—is how many of those women are . . . how to put this politely? *crazy.*

I use the term "crazy" advisedly—and I use it because Kingston herself uses it. It is a brutal term (as we are about to see, Kingston does not shy away from brutal terms for intellectual disability), and it underscores the brutality of what happens to the "village crazy lady" in the book's third section, "Shaman." Kingston introduces her as "an inappropriate woman whom the people stoned" (92); she appears amid a scene of generalized craziness induced by the generalized madness known as war, as the Chinese villagers are "watching for Japanese airplanes that strafed the mountainsides every day" (93):

> The bombing drove people insane. They rolled on the ground, pushed themselves against it, as if the earth could open a door for them. The ones who could not stop shaking after the danger passed would sleep in the cave. My mother explained airplanes to them as she wiggled their ears. (94)

Unfortunately, one day "the village crazy lady put on her headdress with small mirrors" and goes to the river, singing and gamboling and behaving eccentrically. The villagers decide that she is signaling the airplanes to strike; when she is confronted and charged with being a spy, she ill-advisedly answers in the affirmative: "'Yes,' she said, 'I have great powers. I can make the sky rain fire. Me. I did that. Leave me alone or I will do it again'" (95). The villagers respond by battering her head with rocks and stones until she stops breathing.

The Woman Warrior contains many crazy ladies, from Crazy Mary to Moon Orchid to Pee-A-Nah, most of whom are driven into incoherence and madness by the profound injustices that circumscribe their lives. As the narrator remarks toward the end of the book, "I thought every house had to have its crazy woman or crazy girl, every village its idiot. Who would be It at our house? Probably me" (189). It is a testimony to my own obliviousness to disability issues prior to my introduction to disability studies that I managed to teach *The Woman Warrior* in four different classes before I realized that it is a text *about* intellectual disability. Indeed, in the Moon Orchid episode, Kingston explicitly construes intellectual disability as a relation to narrative. The relation is made painfully obvious when Brave Orchid, the narrator's mother, explains that "the difference between mad people and sane people . . . is that sane people have variety when they talk-story. Mad people have only one story that they talk over and over" (159);[12] but it is manifest much earlier, when Moon Orchid first begins her painful descent into madness and incoherence. In its initial stages, her disability is marked by her growing inability to understand what constitutes an appropriate narrative—which is also an index of the degree to which she is becoming an inappropriate woman. For under ordinary circumstances, there is no need to follow one's family members around the house, narrating their every movement and conversation. But Moon Orchid does exactly that, and at one point the text doubles her annoying running commentary:

> The child married to a husband who did not speak Chinese translated for him, "Now she's saying that I'm taking a machine off the shelf and that I'm attaching two metal spiders to it. And she's saying the spiders are spinning with legs intertwined and beating the eggs electrically. Now she says I'm hunting for something in the refrigerator and— ha!—I've found it. I'm taking out butter—'cow oil.' They eat a lot of cow oil,' she is saying." (141)

Moon Orchid's niece is repeating Moon Orchid's obsessive narrative about how the niece is beating eggs; she even repeats Moon Orchid's "ha!" upon her discovery of the butter. But the sentence I want to focus on is "And she's saying the spiders are spinning with legs intertwined and beating the eggs electrically." Surely this is excessive, is it not? It is far too detailed; it is much simpler, and no less accurate, to say "she is beating the eggs" (or perhaps, in a Freudian vein, "an egg is being beaten"). But precisely in its excess, this sentence offers us a striking illustration of how intellectual disability can provide Shklovskian moments of defamiliarization. What is Moon Orchid doing here, what is Kingston doing, but laying bare the device? If Moon Orchid's description of spiders spinning with legs intertwined renews our perception and leads us to see an eggbeater with fresh eyes, to make the stone stony (or the eggbeater eggbeater-y), then one may say that Kingston is deploying intellectual disability as the very vehicle of the literary.[13]

Such moments are compelling in their own right, and should lead readers to see *The Woman Warrior* as a fruitful and fascinating text for disability studies. But they do not go to the question of why I am discussing *The Woman Warrior* under the rubric of "disability as motive." To understand why we should see Kingston's unclassifiable text in the terms I set forth for *Harry Potter and the Deathly Hallows* and *A Wrinkle in Time*, we need to turn to the book's final section, "A Song for a Barbarian Reed Pipe," and to its depictions of the silent girl and the "retarded" boy.

First, our narrator (who seems to bear some passing resemblance to a young Maxine Hong Kingston) writes of a quiet girl in sixth grade, a girl she "hated" (174). In a scene that goes on for an excruciating seven pages, the narrator mercilessly bullies, torments, and physically assaults the girl, trying to force her to talk, calling her "stupid" (177), "dumb," and "a plant" (180). (We are subsequently invited to surmise that the quiet girl is intellectually disabled herself. In later life, her sister and parents take care of her: "she did not have to leave the house except to go to the movies. She was supported. She was protected by her family" [182].) Not long after this encounter, the narrator gets a look at her own school record to date, and learns that "I flunked kindergarten and in first grade had no IQ—a zero IQ" (182–83). And then, later in the section, we are introduced to "a mentally retarded boy who followed me around, probably believing that we were two of a kind" (194). He learns where Kingston's family has its laundry business, and he decides to hang out and haunt the place. At this point, the narrative becomes as brutal as the narrator's treatment of the silent girl. We read that this boy "had an enormous face" and "growled" (194). He gives toys to children: "'Where do you get the toys?' I asked. 'I . . . own . . . stores,' he roared, one word at a time, thick tongued" (195). "Sometimes," Kingston writes, "he chased us—his fat arms out to the side; his fat fingers opening and closing; his legs stiff like Frankenstein's monster, like the mummy dragging its foot" (195). Even his sitting is monstrous, so threatening that it induces the narrator to give up the physical disability—a limp—she had begun to affect:

> Many of the storekeepers invited sitting in their stores, but we did not have sitting because the laundry was hot and because it was outside Chinatown. He sweated; he panted, the stubble rising and falling on his fat neck and chin. He sat on two large cartons that he brought with him and stacked one on top of the other. He said hello to my mother and father, and then, balancing his heavy head, he lowered himself carefully onto his cartons and sat. My parents allowed this. They did not chase him out or comment about how strange he was. I stopped placing orders for toys. I didn't limp anymore; my parents would only figure that this zombie and I were a match.
>
> I studied hard, got straight A's, but nobody seemed to see that I was smart and had nothing in common with this monster, this birth defect. (195)

Nor does it help to try to ignore the intruder: "My back felt sick because it was toward the monster who gave away toys. His lumpishness was sending out germs that would lower my IQ. His leechiness was drawing IQ points out of the back of my head" (196).

Kingston deliberately heightens her narrator's revulsion, but this is difficult material nonetheless; however over-the-top hyperbolic this revulsion may be, it is grounded in a logic of abjection that will be all too familiar to anyone who is acquainted with the social stigma of intellectual disability. And yet this revulsion is crucial to the narrative of the text, not because this man is made to serve as a figure for something else but precisely because he isn't. The narrator is disturbed by this man, and disturbed all the more by the belief—unwarranted, as it turns out—that her parents are considering him as a potential son-in-law. Clearly, the writer who fears becoming the crazy woman or the village idiot would be particularly threatened by the mentally retarded man who draws IQ points from the back of her head. Perhaps the mentally retarded man is even more threatening than the crazy ladies. Certain forms of intellectual disability render people incapable of giving an account of themselves (and I will return to this problem in chapter 3, in my discussion of narrative irony and self-awareness); such people will never come back to themselves after their bout of madness has served its narrative function, as does King Lear's, to such devastating effect. People with significant intellectual disabilities may not even have the capacity to understand what has happened to Lear, just as they do not have the capacity to proclaim that nothing will come of nothing, or to understand the multiple ironies that ripple outward from that utterance. They haunt narrative, as Kingston's retarded man haunts the laundry and Kingston herself, with the insistence on a form of human embodiment that cannot narrate itself—it can only be narrated. And they haunt all narrators with the possibility that perhaps they too, someday, will be unable to tell a coherent story.

Mindedness is so obviously a necessary condition for self-representation and narration that it should be no surprise to find narratives in which various forms of damaged mindedness serve neither as moral barometers of individual persons nor as invitations to pity or horror but as meditations on the very possibility of narrative representation. It is no coincidence that Maxine Hong Kingston's narrator finally explodes at her mother, explaining and justifying herself—"I may be ugly and clumsy, but one thing I'm not, I'm not retarded" (201)—in response to the "mentally retarded" boy's very presence in the text. By this point, the text has firmly, insistently established a relation between intellectual disability and speech, as if the fear of the one necessarily produces the other, as if one begins to narrate partly in order to show—to show to others and to oneself—that one is neither crazy nor retarded. Here, then, the aversion to intellectual disability turns out to be the very motive for Kingston's narrative: *this* is why Kingston's narrator is telling us what her mother told her not to tell anyone.

By contrast, in J. M. Coetzee's *Life and Times of Michael K*, intellectual disability is not only the motive for the narrative but its very predicate: from the novel's opening pages, it subtends every aspect of the life and times of Michael K. He is born with a harelip, which almost immediately comes to signify a more pervasive and character-defining condition of disability:

> Because of his disfigurement and because his mind was not quick, Michael was taken out of school after a short trial and committed to the protection of Huis Norenius in Faure, where at the expense of the state he spent the rest of his childhood in the company of variously other afflicted and unfortunate children learning the elements of reading, writing, counting, sweeping, scrubbing, bedmaking, dishwashing, basketweaving, woodwork and digging. (4)

From Huis Norenius to the work camp Jakkalsdrif to the medical facility in which Michael K spends part 2 of the novel, the novel structures the life and times of Michael K in relation to institutionalization: after the death of Michael's mother early in the book, the plot, if we can call it that, hangs entirely on the question of whether Michael will manage to evade the various state institutions that seem to be all that remains of the fabric of South African society.

It is very tempting to read Michael K as a kind of *Homo sacer* supercrip, the minimal man whose story is narratable only because he manages to escape incarceration twice, eking out a bare existence not on his wits—his mind is not quick—but on his skills as a gardener and as a freelance hunger artist. On that reading—which the book encourages explicitly in the person of the doctor who narrates part 2 and implicitly in the trajectory of the book as a whole—the climactic moment of Michael's narrative appears in this extended passage in the final pages of the novel, in which Michael finally appears capable of a synoptic reading of his own life and times, a vision of the carceral society *in toto*:

At least, he thought, at least I have not been clever, and come back to Sea Point full of stories of how they beat me in the camps till I was thin as a rake and simple in the head. I was mute and stupid in the beginning, I will be mute and stupid at the end. There is nothing to be ashamed of in being simple. They were locking up simpletons before they locked up anyone else. Now they have camps for children whose parents run away, camps for people who kick and foam at the mouth, camps for people with big heads and people with little heads, camps for people with no visible means of support, camps for people chased off the land, camps for people they find living in storm-water drains, camps for street girls, camps for people who can't add two and two, camps for people who forget their papers at home, camps for people who live in the mountains and blow up bridges in the night. Perhaps the truth is that it is enough to be out of the camps, out of all the camps at the same time. Perhaps that is enough of an achievement, for the time being. (182)

This sounds very much indeed like a summation, a what-it-has-all-meant litany placed emphatically at the end of a narrative in which it *has* been enough to be out of the camps, to have avoided every form of biopower, and to have abjured one's humanity altogether in so doing: "What a pity," Michael thinks earlier, "that to live in times like these a man must be ready to live like a beast. . . . A man must live so that he leaves no trace of his living. That is what it has come to" (99). The camps themselves have been predicated on the detection and administration of intellectual disability: *they were locking up simpletons before they locked up anyone else.*

There is nothing wrong with such a reading, of course, unless one leaps from it to the conclusion to which Quayson comes in his chapter on Coetzee—that Michael K simply has autism, and his autism is registered in the text by his silence. This, I think, constitutes a needlessly reductive understanding of Michael K's self-description as "mute and stupid," and a symptom of the pervasive symptomology in disability studies whereby the practice of reading becomes an exercise in finding evidence for the imposition of diagnostic categories. (I will return to this dynamic in my readings of *The Curious Incident of the Dog in the Night-Time*, which invites that kind of diagnostic reading, and *Martian Time-Slip*, whose text is filled with characters diagnosing themselves and each other.) But there is more to be said about Michael K's muteness and stupidity. It is not merely a question of whether those characteristics can be read as symptoms of a condition of disability; it is also a question of what they do to the fabric of the narrative as well as the social fabric of a carceral South Africa. To put this another way, Michael K poses something of a problem for plot and something of a problem for the rendering of interiority: there are passages in *Life and Times of Michael K* that approach the condition of nonnarrative. What is one to do with "a spell of unemployment which he spent lying on his bed looking at his hands" (4), or the "long periods when he sat staring at his hands, his mind blank" (33), or the "spells when he simply stood or knelt before his handiwork, his mind elsewhere" (100)? When Michael leaves Prince Albert and goes off to live in the mountains, his life and times approach the condition of narrative absolute zero: "Now, in front of his cave, he sometimes locked his fingers behind his head, closed his eyes, and emptied his mind, wanting nothing, looking forward to nothing" (69). How does one tell a story that has no temporality and no desire, where disability becomes a motive force that drains the narrative of motive?[14]

This is not merely a technical question, a puzzle for narrative strategy. It informs every aspect of the life and times of Michael K, and *Life and Times of Michael K*. There are moments when Michael adopts what Blakey Vermeule calls "strategic mindblindness," hoping that if he looks "very stupid" (40), he will be exempted from scrutiny at the checkpoints; there are moments when his appearance becomes the basis for charity, as when "the Vrouevereniging ladies, perhaps because he was so thin, perhaps because they had decided he was simple, regularly allowed him to clean the soup-bucket: three time a week this made up his meal" (84), and when the doctor in part 2 decides to try to protect him from the worst of what the camps entail. Only when the doctor takes over the narrative do we learn that Michael's harelip produces a noticeable speech defect, that "he would find it easier to get along if he could talk like everyone else" (131); until then, we are invited to assume that his appearance alone is the basis for how other characters interact with him. "See if he's got a tongue," says one officer (no doubt anticipating the central enigma of Coetzee's next novel, *Foe*, which I will discuss in chapter 3); "see if he is such an idiot as he looks" (122). For every other character in the book, Michael K simply *is* his facial appearance—"how could I forget a face like that?" asks Captain Oosthuizen of Jakkalsdrif—and his facial appearance signifies intellectual disability. There is nothing else one needs to know, and even when the narrative gives us access to what interiority Michael K may be said to possess, we find that his mind is a blank: "*There is nothing there,* I'm telling you," says the doctor to Noël, the camp director, "and if you handed him over to the police they would come to the same conclusion: there is nothing there, no story of the slightest interest to rational people" (142).

It is worth asking, then, why we are bothering to read about the life and times of Michael K in the first place. If indeed his existence is summed up by his disability, then we could have stopped after the first four or five paragraphs: after we learn that his mind is not quick, we proceed to learn that his mind is often a blank. That is not a story. And yet Michael's storylessness is itself narratable, and that dynamic, too, has implications both for narrative technique and for plot. Michael is a challenge for a novelist who wants to employ free indirect discourse or any other device for revealing a character's interiority, as the novel openly acknowledges: "Always, when he tried to explain himself to himself, there remained a gap, a hole, a darkness before which his understanding baulked, into which it was useless to pour words. The words were eaten up, the gap remained. His was always a story with a hole in it: a wrong story, always wrong" (110). That gap structures the text, beginning with the gap that defines Michael's facial features and extending to the gap that is part 2, the hole in Michael's story that is filled by the doctor's narrative of Michael K.[15] But he is also a challenge to the authorities who apprehend him (in at least two senses of "apprehend"): because he cannot tell a coherent story of his own, one will be supplied to him, and (with one exception) this will never be a benevolent exercise. "Tell me your story," demands the officer who apprehends him in his garden at the Visagie house (122), and this is not an invitation for Michael to sit for a spell and relate his life and times. This is an order, issued by someone who is convinced that Michael K is aiding and abetting an insurrection. At various points in the novel Michael is assigned identities to supplement the baseline assumption that he is an idiot: he is a drunk, he is a vagrant, he is a terrorist. His attempts to evade the camps, then, to evade the authorities, amount to attempts to evade being assigned those narratives, attempts to evade narrative altogether.

Those who cannot represent themselves must be represented: this is an imperative that runs from the political conundrum of Marx's *Eighteenth Brumaire* to the ethical demands attendant on any attempt to administer intellectual disability, and it is the key, as well, to Quayson's sense of disability as hermeneutical impasse. Once we understand that Michael K's desire is to avoid the camps, we have a story to tell; once we understand that Michael K also desires to avoid *being narrated*, we have a more problematic story to tell. For one thing, this realization should caution us away from the reading of Michael K as *Homo sacer* supercrip, the Man Who Escaped the Camps, precisely because this is the reading offered intratextually by the doctor himself, at the close of part 2 when he addresses a hypothetical Michael K, standing in for the Michael who has escaped: "Your stay in the camp was merely an allegory, if you know that word. It was an allegory—speaking at the highest level—of how scandalously, how outrageously a meaning can take up residence in a system without becoming a term in it. Did you not notice how, whenever I tried to pin you down, you slipped away?" (166). It should not escape notice that this utterance, too, constitutes an attempt to pin Michael down after he has slipped away, albeit a meta-attempt to assign him not an identity (drunk, vagrant, terrorist, idiot) but a narrative function, that of a meaning that does not become a term. (And the meta-attempt is admirably opaque: we may be familiar with terms that do not become meanings; but how does a meaning fail to become a term?) Again, it is very tempting to take this passage as the definitive statement of What Michael K Means, just as it is tempting to read the closing "camps" passage as What *Michael K* Means. And again, there is nothing wrong with such a reading: it is plausible enough, as readings of people (or texts) go, and it is benevolent in a way no other "apprehension" of Michael is, insofar as it is the basis for the doctor's kindness. But it is still an apprehension, and it is still an apprehension whose condition of possibility is Michael's incarceration.

This is not to say that whoever "reads" Michael K thereby jails him, or is complicit with people who do. Things are just not that simple—or that allegorical. It is to say that our apprehension of Michael K, and of *Michael K*, entails interpretive protocols and dilemmas that go well beyond the obvious—intellectual disability as hermeneutical impasse (what does Michael K mean?), intellectual disability as null set and/or moral test (how should Michael K be treated?). Those dynamics are at work in any engagement with Michael K and *Michael K*, to be sure. But Michael K's disabled relation to narrative also has implications for narrative itself, as the closing ironic turn of one of the doctor's readings of Michael suggests:

We have all tumbled over the lip into the cauldron of history: only you, following your idiot light, biding your time in an orphanage (who would have thought of *that* as a hiding-place?), evading the peace and the war, skulking in the open where no one dreamed of looking, have managed to live in the old way, drifting through time, observing the seasons, no more trying to change the course of history than a grain of sand does. We ought to value you and celebrate you, we ought to put your clothes on a maquette in a museum, your clothes and your packet of pumpkin seeds too, with a label; there ought to be a plaque nailed to the racetrack wall commemorating your stay here. But that is not the way it is going to be. The truth is that you are going to perish in obscurity and be buried in a nameless hole in a corner of the racecourse, transport to the acres of Woltemade being out of the question nowadays, and no one is going to remember you but me, unless you yield and at last open your mouth. I appeal to you, Michaels: *yield!* (151 52)

This is unquestionably a more benevolent demand for Michael's story than that of any arresting officer (though the doctor takes the name "Michaels" from the account filed by the arresting officer, who reports that Michael K, whom he calls Michaels, is an "arsonist" [131]). But it is still a demand: no one will remember you unless you open your mouth. And yet what the doctor does not know—cannot know, without breaking the frame of reference of the narrative he inhabits—is that Michael K will not be forgotten, any more than the exploits of Don Quixote will (although, as we will see, *Don Quixote* establishes a relation between narrative and intellectual disability that does depend on the breaking of the fictional frame): his life and times are being narrated, conveyed in a book called *Life and Times of Michael K.* In other words, Michael K has managed to elude all forms of representation except for those of the narrative he inhabits, the one in which we read of his elusiveness and unrepresentability. His intellectual disability thus becomes the impetus not only for the narrative of his life, and of every character's interaction with him, but also for all interpretive procedures brought to bear on him; and Coetzee cannily, disturbingly, insistently suggests that such procedures include those of the novel itself. *Life and Times of Michael K* thereby stands not merely as a representation or thematization of intellectual disability but rather as a virtuoso examination of intellectual disability as motive, a rendering of intellectual disability as the condition of possibility for the text and its apprehension by readers. In the following chapter, we will see how this narrative strategy becomes a vehicle for literary techniques that open onto radical forms of alterity, by way of radical experiments with the fabric of time.

CHAPTER TWO

Time

The first section of *The Sound and the Fury* is not hard to read. No, really. I invite you, dear reader, as I once invited my son Nick, to take a crack at it:

> Through the fence, between the curling flower spaces, I could see them hitting. They were coming toward where the flag was and I went along the fence. Luster was hunting in the grass by the flower tree. They took the flag out, and they were hitting. Then they put the flag back and they went to the table, and he hit and the other hit. Then they went on, and I went along the fence. Luster came away from the flower tree and we went along the fence and they stopped and we stopped and I looked through the fence while Luster was hunting in the grass. (3)

There isn't a single complex sentence in that memorable opening paragraph, or in the section as a whole; there are no punctuation marks other than commas and periods (certainly no semicolons or parentheses, as here).[1] Neither the syntax nor the vocabulary would strain any reader proficient at the third-grade reading level. So what, precisely, is all the fuss about? Why do college students howl with dismay (as mine have, every time I have dared to assign the novel in an American literature survey) when they are asked to read the section without the help of textual aids? Compare that simple paragraph to this one, which is written in precisely the same mode:

> Ineluctable modality of the visible: at least that if no more, thought through my eyes. Signatures of all things I am here to read, seaspawn and seawrack: the nearing tide, that rusty boot. Snotgreen, bluesilver, rust: coloured signs. Limits of the diaphane. But he adds: in bodies. Then he was aware of them bodies before of them coloured. How? By knocking his sconce against them, sure. Go easy. Bald he was and a millionaire, *maestro di color che sanno*. Limit of the diaphane in. Why in? Diaphane, adiaphane. If you can put your five fingers through it, it is a gate, if not a door. Shut your eyes and see. (Joyce 37)

This is rough going for a couple of reasons. The word "diaphane," the allusion to Dante in the original (and how did you know it was Dante? be honest, now), and the (implicit) reference to Aristotle as "he" in the fifth sentence: a reader has to know a great deal in order to make her way through the thicket of Stephen Dedalus's narrative, and has to learn how to navigate its idiosyncratic syntax, incomplete sentences, and cognitive leaps. As a result, very few and far between are the brave souls who attempt to read *Ulysses* without the assistance of a good reader's guide (my own was Harry Blamires's *Bloomsday Book*).

It would appear that I've stacked the deck at the outset of this chapter, by contrasting the stream of consciousness of an adult with a significant intellectual disability with that of one of the most aggressively hyperintellectual characters in the history of literature. Clearly, the transcription of Benjy Compson's mental events, as he watches the golfers play in what used to be "his" pasture, is easier to read than Stephen Dedalus's ruminations on sight because Benjy's mental capacity is so much more limited than Stephen's. And yet Benjy's narrative as a whole is not easy to read, even though, sentence by sentence, it's a breeze. Why? Is it because Benjy does not know enough to use the words most people familiar with golf would have used, such as green, tee (for "table"), or putting (for "hitting")? Benjy's lack of familiarity with golf doesn't help matters, but the task of figuring out what's going on in that paragraph isn't a significant burden compared to the demands made by the section as a whole. The real problem, as is evident to everyone who picks up the book, is that Benjy Compson has a sense of time that does not make sense to us. His narrative thus lacks some of the necessary connective tissue that makes narrative intelligible as narrative.

Benjy's narrative is not incoherent, it is not unintelligible; after only a few pages, even the most befuddled reader can get the sense that Benjy is relaying a sequence of episodes from his life, though that sequence is far from clear. But his narrative itself is disabled, in the sense I have employed in calling the narrative of the film *Memento* "disabled" (Bérubé 2005b): some of (what we take to be) the ordinary functions of narrative are here inoperative. In the case of *Memento*, I argue that there is no way to reconcile *fabula* and *szujet*, no way to reconstruct a straightforward narrative progression even after one "compensates" for the fact that the latter is relayed backward in time and focalized through a person with no short-term memory.[2] Benjy's chapter is not quite so radical, inasmuch as it is ultimately possible to piece together a coherent *fabula* from the unfolding of the *szujet*— though as we will see, this involves some significant interpretive assumptions along the way (most significantly in the "bluegum chillen" passage). I could say the same, *mutatis mutandis*, about the "Circe" chapter of *Ulysses*: it is a tour de force, one of the most extraordinary things written in English, but it is not a narrative. It is what happens, according to Joyce, when narrative falls asleep and some other logic takes over. It does not contain any characters with intellectual disabilities, so the issues raised by its experimental form are not quite what they are in Benjy's chapter; but when the narrative in question *is* conveyed by a character with an intellectual disability, then one question becomes paramount: what does his or her disability tell us about the functions of time and narrative in general? That is, what do we learn about the ways narrative time works by reading narratives in which some of the functions of time in narrative do not appear to work as we expect?

There is another question lurking here, but I want to postpone it for the following chapter, when it can be discussed in (what I hope will be) the more fruitful context of textual self-awareness. Because Faulkner's brilliant formal experiment is attributed to the workings of an individual character's subjectivity (obviously, it did not need to be framed this way; Joyce's "Circe" chapter is not tethered in this way), we are implicitly asked to try to determine the extent to which the character with an intellectual disability has the capacity to understand the narrative he or she inhabits. We know, for example, that Benjy does not understand why he has been "gelded," and that he knows nothing about the administration of disability in his world, in the era of institutionalization and involuntary sterilization. We think we know that Benjy experiences his loss as loss, and that he connects it to other losses, as in this juxtaposition between the scene of Damuddy's death and the scene in which Benjy sees his castrated body, a juxtaposition enabled by the associations that accompany undressing:

> Quentin and Versh came in. Quentin had his face turned away. "What are you crying for." Caddy said.
> "Hush." Dilsey said. "You all get undressed, now. You can go on home, Versh."

I got undressed and I looked at myself, and I began to cry. Hush,
Luster said. Looking for them aint going to do no good. They're gone.
You keep on like this, and we aint going have you no more birthday. He
put my gown on. (73–74)

Faulkner's appendix to the novel, notoriously, will challenge even this
minimalist reading of Benjy's degree of self-awareness, denying that
he has any substantial sense of what his losses entail: "He could not
remember his sister but only the loss of her" (340), we are told, and
"As with his sister, he remembered not the pasture but only its loss"
(341). But there are good reasons, both theoretical and practical, to
resist Faulkner's characterization of the character he created.[3]

To take the theoretical objection first: as Faulkner himself suggested when he declared that his appendix was "the key to the whole
book," the document presents readers with the overwhelming temptation to take it as The Instructor's Edition, the explanatory device
that clarifies all ambiguities and fleshes out all backstories (including
those of characters who never appear in the book). The appendix thus
invites us to read it as *The Fabula Newsletter*, smoothing out temporal and hermeneutical impasses and giving us the straight story from
start to finish. It is an invitation best resisted, unless we want (and I
hope you will not) to invoke the figure of the author in Foucauldian
terms, that is, as "the ideological figure by which one marks the manner in which we fear the proliferation of meaning" (118), the device
that gets hauled out to determine which interpretations can be said to
be properly "authorized." The practical objection leads us back to the
text of Benjy's section in such a way that the question, *Mr. Faulkner,*
did you actually read your book? is not altogether impudent. I do not
understand how any reader of the opening scene of the novel can
claim that Benjy does not remember his pasture; his moaning and his
mourning are occasioned precisely by his proximity to the pasture,

and both are intensified by the sound of golfers calling for their cad-
dies. The fact that Luster understands the homophone only in order
to torment Benjy further—"'You want something to beller about. All
right, then. Caddy.' he whispered. 'Caddy. Beller now. Caddy'" (55)—
is surely not to be referred to the limitations associated with Benjy's
form of intellectual disability, but to the other characters' failures of
sympathetic imagination.[4]

In this respect, the "bluegum chillen" passage is perhaps the most
important of the transitions in Benjy's section, insofar as the logic behind the transition seems more obscure than any other juxtaposition
in the novel. The passage reads as follows, and it appears just after the
scene in which Benjy intuits that Caddy has lost her virginity:

> *Versh said, Your name Benjamin now. You know how come your name
> Benjamin now. They making a bluegum out of you. Mammy say in old
> time your granpaw changed nigger's name, and he turn preacher, and
> when they look at him, he bluegum too. Didn't use to be bluegum, nei-
> ther. And when family woman look him in the eye in the full of the
> moon, chile born bluegum. And one evening, when they was about a
> dozen them bluegum chillen running around the place, he never come
> home. Possum hunters found him in the woods, et clean. And you know
> who et him. Them bluegum chillen did.* (69)

Why should this unsettling and difficult piece of folklore, conveyed by
Versh, follow the moment in 1909 in which Caddy runs into the house
crying? There is a name change involved here, yes, but the rest of the
tale is disturbingly unrelated to Benjy, who presumably is not going to
become bluegum or join together with other bluegum children to eat
any bluegum preachers in the woods. Most of Benjy's transitions are
much more straightforward, involving key words, place associations,
or memories of getting snagged on a nail. That is why Benjy is usually

considered a passive recorder of scenes and sense impressions; his narrative does not seem to be motivated consciously, and Faulkner makes no attempt to explain how Benjy's words got onto the page. They are apparently direct transcriptions of mental events, in stream-of-consciousness mode. As Stacy Burton has written, "Benjy narrates, but critics have tended to respond to the challenge of his puzzling discourse by seeing it as Faulkner's formal experiment rather than as Benjy's narrative" (214). We need, therefore, to contrast the strategy of this formal experiment with that of Daniel Keyes in *Flowers for Algernon* or Mark Haddon in *The Curious Incident of the Dog in the Night-Time*, who are exceptionally careful to explain how their intellectually disabled narrators happen to be writing a book; contrast it also with Quentin and Jason, who seem to be standard first-person narrators aware (acutely aware, in Jason's case) that they are telling a story (even if, in Quentin's section, we feel as if we are overhearing someone's thoughts, whereas Jason, from his opening sentence, has a very vivid sense of his implied reader).

But Richard Godden argues that Benjy does indeed have a plan here, and that, after his fashion, he is consciously plotting:

> The complexity of the analogy realizes a childishly simplistic purpose: Benjy wants his small sister for himself, and to that end has engaged in "plotting," inventing a temporal comparison that allows him to move from an unpleasant event in 1909 to an earlier but less troubling loss. The shift works for him because, as a bluegum, Benjy can control his sister's sexuality. My attribution of an act of consciousness to Benjy—a character most typically described as "passive and uncomprehending" or "totally devoid of . . . consciousness" at a pattern-making level— stems from a conviction that even those with severe learning disabilities are liable to whatever subterranean stories characterize the culture within which they pass their long childhoods. (101–2)

I wouldn't put things this way myself; it is not clear, for one thing, why Caddy should be considered "small," and I don't think Benjy is merely "liable" to the "subterranean stories" he hears in the course of his "long childhood" (which itself is too close to the infantilizing remark that Benjy "been three years old thirty years" [17]). But Godden is right in principle to entertain the possibility that Benjy is "inventing a temporal comparison that allows him to move from an unpleasant event in 1909 to an earlier but less troubling loss"; the key word here, of course, is "inventing," and the suggestion is that Benjy not only has some conscious control over the sequence of events in his narrative but also has something we might want to call an unconscious, as well—an unconscious more unruly and elaborate than that of a three-year-old.

I don't want to make more of this possibility than the text allows; we cannot go so far as to say that Benjy has the capacity to think to himself, "Dang, I wish I weren't so sad that Caddy has been banned from the house," or, more elaborately, "I wish my mother and Jason had not banned Caddy from the house—that really seems excessive, especially since her daughter is being raised here." But there is an important side issue at stake in the claim that Benjy has some idea of what he is doing by associating Caddy's sexuality with the bluegum story. It is one thing if Quentin and Jason tie themselves into knots about Compson honor and the ideology of Southern white womanhood; this is a key feature of their narratives, whereby they begin to lose the thread and spiral into reverie and/or incoherence whenever Caddy's (or, in Jason's case, Caddy's and her daughter Quentin's) sexuality is the narrative focus, and we can attribute their obsessions to their conscious and unconscious desires, or, if you prefer (though it comes to much the same thing), their interpellation by the standard old-Southern ideologies of gender and race. But if *Benjy*, simple innocent Benjy (as readers, beginning with his creator, have cast him), objects to Caddy wearing perfume and kissing boys, one is tempted to think that there really is something wrong about it all, and that Caddy's sexuality is a problem simply because it is Caddy's sexuality. One is tempted to naturalize the pathologization of her sexuality, in precisely the way the muddy-drawers scene invites us to do (OMG Caddy's private parts are dirty and always were, even when she was little), or in the way Caddy herself seems to do when she says, *"There was something terrible in me sometimes at night I could see it grinning at me I could see it through them grinning at me through their faces"* (112). But if Benjy's narrative trajectory is motivated in some way, then he becomes an interested party alongside his brothers, such that we can say, *Well, if Benjy is upset by the smell of Caddy's perfume, that's just Benjy's take on things—it's not like he gives us direct unmediated narrative access to the things themselves.*

There are, after all, two salient reasons why Benjy might worry about Caddy wearing perfume, kissing boys, and losing her virginity: one is that he has a version of Quentin's concern about the family honor, and both brothers' extreme squickiness about female sexuality in general. The other is that he has a vague but well-grounded sense that if Caddy wears perfume and kisses boys and has sex (I imagine that it is immaterial to him whether it is premarital or sanctioned by church/state union), then eventually she will leave the Compson home and he will lose the only family member who has any substantial notion that he has a subjectivity worth attending to. The point of putting interpretive pressure on the bluegum passage, then, is that it allows us not only to entertain the possibility that Benjy has some kind of sifting and sorting mechanism that explains his temporal leaps as involving something more complicated than mere sensory associations, but also to suggest that Benjy's relation to time opens out onto questions that go well beyond our determination of the limits of his subjectivity.

For the larger point is that Benjy's text makes it quite clear that Benjy has a rich interior life, full of acute sensations, vivid associations, and inchoate emotions that are revealed in subtle and achronological ways; his emotions may be more inchoate, perhaps, than yours or mine (or Quentin's or Jason's, though this is arguable), but the difference is a matter of degree rather than kind. The question is whether he *knows* he has a rich interior life, whether he is capable of self-reflection. I will take up the question of textual self-awareness in the following chapter; here, I want to stress one of its implications for Faulkner's experiment with narrative temporality. The device of Benjy's section is that there is no device: the assumption, once again, is that the narrative is simply the index and register of the way Benjy perceives the world, just as the "Proteus" chapter of *Ulysses* gives us the index and register of the way Dedalus muses on visuality and Aristotle and the limits of the diaphane. It is a truism of Faulkner criticism that Benjy's section offers a kind of overture to the novel, a synoptic rendering of its major motifs (inexpressible loss, Caddy's sexuality and the perils of the femme fatale, the decline of the old Southern aristocracy, Caddy's sexuality and the ideology of Southern white womanhood, death and order and the sense of an ending, Caddy's sexuality and Caddy's sexuality) that provides something like a translation of the Compson narrative into what Joseph Frank brilliantly called "spatial form in modern literature."[5] But what does it mean that Faulkner orchestrates such an overture by rendering it *precisely as an artifact of intellectual disability*, particularly since there is no intellectual disability known to humankind that would lead someone to perceive the world as Benjy does?

In Benjy's case, the gambit is something like this: here is a person whose perception of the world does not depend on the ordinary narrative logic of "The king died and then the queen died of grief." Rather, his perception of the world is something more like "The cows came jumping out of the barn at Caddy's wedding so loss of Caddy, who will take care of me? Damuddy died and Caddy was in the tree, and the day Caddy wore perfume now there is a guy with a red tie in my yard hitting on Caddy's daughter Quentin, and another time Caddy smelled like rain." There are two important theoretical principles at work here. The first involves something I mentioned at the close of the introduction: this is a *fictional disability*, not only in the sense that it is a disability that is wholly "made up," that does not exist in the DSM-5 (or any of its precursors), but also (and more important, for readers of *The Sound and the Fury* and viewers of *Memento*) in the sense that it is a disability that manifests itself as a relation to the structure of fiction. The second is that there is something we might call, if we arranged a shotgun marriage between the work of Paul Ricoeur and Mikhail Bakhtin, an *intellectual disability chronotope* at work here, by which narrative marks its relation to intellectual disability precisely by rendering intellectual disability as a productive and illuminating derangement of ordinary protocols of narrative temporality.

In volume 1 of *Time and Narrative*, Ricoeur writes, "Time becomes human to the extent that it is articulated through a narrative mode, and narrative attains its full meaning when it becomes a condition of temporal existence" (52). This is a fundamental insight, properly insisting on the double-helix interweaving of narrative and temporal existence; in retrospect, it is somewhat astonishing how much work Ricoeur had to do to blend Aristotle and Augustine in order to achieve this insight, painstakingly countering structuralism's indifference to chronology and consequent flattening out of narrative theory. (By contrast, Frank Kermode, less harried by structuralism and its Continental pedigree, simply suggested that traditional narrative takes the form of "tick-tock," and presto, his narrative theory emphasized temporality.) One reason that narrative experiments with time might involve characters with intellectual disabilities is that in exploring alternative modes of temporal existence, we are exploring not only the variety of humans' relations to time but also the ways time itself can "become human." Among the most appalling discoveries of the past century, after all, involves the realization that time, like space, only gets weirder and more unfathomable the more closely one looks at it.[6] Perhaps, in this respect, Augustine foresaw the future of human attempts to understand time: "What, then, is time? I know well enough what it is, provided that nobody asks me; but if I am asked what it is and try to explain, I am baffled. . . . [W]e cannot rightly say that time *is*, except by reason of its impending state of *not being*" (264). I made a version of this observation to Jamie one morning when we were late for something (he was in his mid-teens), remarking that although we are surrounded by clocks and reasonably conscious of the Earth's rotation and revolution around the sun, we really don't know what time is or why it only goes forward, to which he promptly replied, "Except in *Harry Potter*, with Hermione's Time-Turner," whereupon I nearly crashed the car in surprise. But of course he is right: fiction is where we can imagine such things as time travel, precognition, and alternate temporal dimensions—and where we (and Jamie) can speculate on the existence of many kinds of disability chronotopes, as well.

Indeed, as we will see in the course of this chapter, the deployment of intellectual disability in narrative can serve to expand (or, if you decide that the experiments in this vein are ultimately unsuccessful, merely to *try to* expand) the domain of narrative literature beyond the boundaries of human experience altogether. In *The Sound and the Fury*, there is the possibility that Benjy's perpetual present allows indirectly for a perception of the sacred, at least for Dilsey; in Woolf's *Mrs. Dalloway*, Powers's *Echo Maker*, and Dick's *Martian Time-Slip* (to which I will turn first), the disability chronotope offers an outlet into realms of temporal experience that exceed human perception, bringing animal consciousness and/or geological time into play.

* * *

I have assumed, so far, a general readerly familiarity with the novels I have discussed, believing there is no reason at this point in the history of professional literary criticism to offer synoptic introductions to *The Sound and the Fury*, *The Woman Warrior*, *Life and Times of Michael K*, or the Harry Potter series. In the case of Philip K. Dick's little-known and rarely studied *Martian Time-Slip*, however, I suspect that an introduction is in order, at least for readers who are not level-six PKD fans.

The premise of *Martian Time-Slip* (1964) sounds like one of Dick's standard—that is, "standard" in the sense of "inconceivably odd"— variations on postwar American science fiction. It is 1994, and the inhabitants of a polluted, radioactive Earth have colonized Mars under the auspices of the United Nations. The colonization project is complicated by (a) the fact that Mars has humanoid inhabitants who are closely related to early human hominids and constitute a dying race of aboriginal hunter-gatherers (they are black, they are called Bleekmen, and are despised, reviled, and employed as domestic servants); and (b) the expense of shipping heavy machinery to Mars, which means that a great deal of the colonists' infrastructure is already beginning to decay. Accordingly, repairmen are in such high demand that they have become a prestigious class of professionals (psychiatrists, by contrast, have to eke out a living by trolling for clients), and one of the most important power brokers on the planet is one Arnie Kott, Supreme Goodmember of the Water Workers' Local, Fourth Planet Branch. Much of the narrative seems to be third-person nonparticipant omniscient, focalized through Kott or through the repairman Jack Bohlen, with liberal use of free indirect discourse; the novel's early chapters include a narrative focalized through an herbal foods and black market salesman named Norbert Steiner, but after he commits suicide, the novel drops him from the narrative trajectory. Steiner's son, Manfred, is on the autism spectrum, such as it was understood in 1964. He is housed in the only Martian facility open to him and other "anomalous" children, a school known as Camp Ben-Gurion, run by the Israeli settlement on Mars. Early in the novel, we learn that the United Nations is considering a bill that would close Camp B-G, as it is known, because (in the words of Anne Esterhazy, the mother of an "anomalous" child and the ex-wife of Arnie Kott)

> they don't want to see what they call "defective stock" appearing on the colonial planets. . . . Back Home they see the existence of anomalous children on Mars as a sign that one of Earth's major problems has been transplanted into the future, because we are the future, to them. (41–42)

Clearly, Dick's novel foregrounds questions of race and eugenics, colonization, and disability: "Earth's major problems," indeed. If that were all there is to say about *Martian Time-Slip*, then one could plausibly file it under the (capacious) heading of works of speculative fiction that address Real Social Problems in especially fanciful ways, and one could praise it for being on the side of the angels, who know a genocidal, eugenic program when they see one. But the novel is—happily, and vexatiously—far more complex than that. For it appears that Manfred Steiner inhabits a realm of narrative time that not only exceeds that of any character in the novel, but also warps and distorts the narrative fabric of *Martian Time-Slip* itself. One of Manfred's supervisors, a Dr. Glaub, tells Manfred's father, Norbert, of a "new theory about autism" (46) that has recently been developed by Swiss researchers. The theory, in fine, is that people with autism experience a different sense of time than neurotypicals, such that they perceive the world around them moving at a rate too fast for them to process. This then accounts for their "withdrawal," their inability to socialize or read affective cues. It turns out that the Swiss theory is partly right: Manfred Steiner does indeed live in a different sense of time than the novel's other characters. But his withdrawal from the world is occasioned only partly by that fact; more immediately, he is haunted by visions of the inevitable decay of everything around him. He can see the far future, in which even Martian structures yet unbuilt have fallen into disrepair and desuetude ("gubbish," the pervasive term for garbage/rubbish that runs throughout the novel). He is particularly horrified by a recurring vision of himself at the age of two hundred, having been immobilized for decades and kept alive (and thoroughly neglected) in the medical facility of a huge housing complex, even after his limbs have been amputated and most of his internal organs have been removed.

Arnie Kott, upon hearing that people with autism might be "precogs" who have access to the future, hires Jack Bohlen to build a device that can bridge different senses of narrative time and translate Manfred's visions into a readable form in the present. Kott's motivation is almost comically petty: he wants access to information about a blockbuster real estate deal involving a nearby Martian mountain range, the remote and barren F.D.R. Mountains. The denouement of that plot occurs when Bohlen has to break the news to Kott that (a) Manfred has drawn a detailed sketch of the decay of the massive AM-WEB housing project housed in the mountains (over a century in the future), and (b) his own father, Leo Bohlen, has already bought the land in question. Kott is an imperious man, and Bohlen is consumed with anxiety at the prospect of telling him that his experiment

with time translation does not work (since Manfred is no use for giving insider-trading tips) and that the point of the enterprise is moot
anyway.

On the way to that denouement, however, the novel becomes seriously weird. The scene in which Bohlen breaks the news to Kott is
narrated four times; the first three are out of sequence (that is, they
are effectively a series of flash-forwards), and though each seems to
be focalized through Manfred, and is announced by a paragraph that
begins, "Inside Mr. Kott's skin were dead bones, shiny and wet" (157,
167, 178), the three scenes are nevertheless narrated from different
spatial perspectives (we follow a character out of the living room in
one, but stay in the living room in another) and are marked by subtle
differences from episode to episode. The first two episodes appear in
chapter 10, but then chapter 11 opens with the third, as if chapter 10 is
repeating itself; the subtle differences between the passages read like
"glitches," in the sense that gamers use the term—slight but deliberate
deviations from the code.[7] Two examples follow; the first compares
passages from the second and third flash-forward episodes, and the
second compares passages from all three:

> Jack Bohlen, too, was a dead sack, teeming with gubbish. The outside
> that fooled almost everyone, it was painted pretty and smelled good,
> bent down over Miss Anderton, and he saw that; he saw it wanting her
> in an awful fashion. It poured its wet, sticky self to her and the dead
> bug words popped from its mouth. "I love Mozart," Mr. Kott was say-
> ing. "I'll put this tape on." (167)

> Jack Bohlen, too, was a dead sack, teeming with gubbish. The outside
> that fooled almost everyone, it was painted pretty and smelled good,
> bent down over Miss Anderton, and he saw that; he saw it wanting her
> in a filthy fashion. It poured its wet, sticky self nearer and nearer to her

and the dead bug words popped from its mouth and fell on her. The dead bug words scampered off into the folds of her clothing, and some squeezed into her skin and entered her body. "I love Mozart," Mr. Kott said. "I'll put this tape on." (177)

Both seem to be narrated from Manfred's perspective, mixing his idiosyncratic vision of his fellow creatures with ordinary dialogue. The second series of examples, however, introduces another level of complexity and perplexity. When Kott puts on the tape, it turns out not to be Mozart but one of his electronically coded messages to his confederates:

A hideous racket of screeches and shrieks issued from the speakers, like the convulsions of corpses. Mr. Kott shut off the tape transport. (157)

A hideous racket of screeches and shrieks issued from the speakers, like the convulsions of corpses. He shut off the tape transport. (167)

A hideous racket of screeches and shrieks issued from somewhere in the room, and after a time she realized that it was her; she was convulsed from within, all the corpse-things in her were heaving and crawling, struggling out into the light of the room. God, how could she stop them? They emerged from her pores and scuttled off, dropping from strands of gummy web onto the floor, to disappear into the cracks between the boards. (177–78)

Again, the first two accounts of the "Mozart" tape seem to be focalized by way of Manfred; but the third is quite clearly focalized through the character of Doreen Anderton, who now seems to be overwhelmed by something very much like the "dead bug words" that had poured on her from Bohlen's mouth. Time is not the only thing being warped here; the entire narrative fabric is twisting. Just as, in a later chapter, we are told that "Manfred Steiner's presence had invaded the structure of the Public School, penetrated its deepest being" (194), thereby deranging all the android teachers in the school, here Steiner's presence and perspective somehow "leak" into other characters. The result is that it is finally impossible to attribute these passages solely to Steiner. When, for instance, the confrontation with Kott is finally narrated in "real" time (that is, as an event following the other events of the day in proper temporal sequence) and Kott puts on the Mozart tape, we find that the character who likens the screeches to the convulsions of corpses is Kott himself:

> A hideous racket of screeches and shrieks issued from the speakers. Noises like the convulsions of the dead, *Arnie thought in horror*. He ran to shut off the tape transport. (208; emphasis added)

To whom, then, are we supposed to attribute the thought "noises like the convulsions of the dead" in the three previous versions of this passage? Who or what had access to Arnie's simile, and how did Doreen Anderton, in the third repetition, manage to "realize" that the noises were coming from her?

As for Bohlen, himself a recovered (or recovering?) schizophrenic, he finds himself increasingly incapacitated in the course of the evening; on one page he feels "the coming apart of every piece of his body" (211), and on the next the confrontation and the crisis have passed and he has no recollection of them: "the next thing he knew he was standing on a black, empty sidewalk" (212). In the following chapter, on the following day, Bohlen stops to reflect on what has happened to him and to the novel:

> He had sat, he realized, in Arnie Kott's living room again and again, experiencing that evening before it arrived; and then, when at last it

had taken place in actuality, he had bypassed it. The fundamental disturbance in time-sense, which Dr. Glaub believed was the basis for schizophrenia, was now harassing him. That evening at Arnie's had taken place, and had existed for him . . . but out of sequence. (219–20)

This is a fair enough summary of what we, as readers, have just experienced. So maybe Jack, rather than Manfred, is "responsible" for these out-of-joint and out-of-sequence time-slips. But this hypothesis doesn't solve everything, because the perspective from which Jack Bohlen was a dead sack, teeming with "gubbish" and leering at Doreen Anderton, was clearly not Jack Bohlen's. Manfred's "autistic" rendering of events becomes the "schizophrenic" break in the text of the novel itself. What Dick has crafted in *Martian Time-Slip*—and it is no mean feat—is not merely the depiction of a character whose intellectual disability, like Benjy Compson's, entails a radically different sense of time and narrative; it is also a textualization of that character's intellectual disability such that the character's sense of time and narrative so pervades and structures the novel that it can no longer be attributed to that character's private stream of consciousness.

The other characters' response to the night of the time-slips makes this clear, inasmuch as we can say that anything about this extended episode can be made clear. It is not merely that Manfred warps Jack's sense of time; Doreen also reports having her subjectivity invaded and altered. "I really couldn't stand that child," she tells Jack. "Last night was a nightmare—I kept feeling awful cold squishy tendrils drifting around the room and in my mind . . . intimations of filth and evil that didn't seem to be either in me or outside me—just nearby" (221–22). Doreen is no doubt referring to the corpse-things heaving and crawling in her, but it turns out that even Arnie himself has felt the effects, underscoring Doreen's sense that the phenomenon was neither inside her nor outside her (or, possibly, that her outside was in and her inside was out). In an extended conversation with his Bleekman servant Heliogabalus, in which Heliogabalus not only explains that Manfred's thoughts "are as clear as plastic to me, and mine likewise to him" (226) (thereby revealing that Arnie's plans for Jack's translation device were needless) but also conveys the entire content of Manfred's vision of AM-WEB (to which I will return), Arnie offers yet another theory of what happened on the night of the time-slips:

> "You know what I think?" Arnie said. "I think he does more than just see into time. I think he controls time."
>
> The Bleekman's eyes became opaque. He shrugged.
>
> "Doesn't he?" Arnie persisted. "Listen, Heliogabalus, you black bastard, this kid fooled around with last night. I know it. He saw it in advance and he tried to tamper with it. Was he trying to make it not happen? He was trying to halt time."
>
> "Perhaps," Helio said. (227)

Perhaps. And perhaps everything will make sense when the novel finally gives us Manfred's perspective on the evening, since Manfred allegedly controls time. Or perhaps Manfred's version will turn out to be shockingly, disappointingly ordinary, clearly marked *as* Manfred's, with no traces of bug words or decaying women or strange temporal distortions:

> Seated on the carpet, snipping pictures from the magazines with his scissors and pasting them into new configurations, Manfred Steiner heard the noise and glanced up. He saw Mr. Kott hurry to the tape machine to shut it off. How blurred Mr. Kott became, Manfred noticed. It was hard to see him when he moved so swiftly; it was as if in some way he had managed to disappear from the room and then reappear in another spot. The boy felt frightened.

The noise, too, frightened him. He looked to the couch where Mr. Bohlen sat, to see if he were upset. But Mr. Bohlen remained where he was with Doreen Anderton, interlinked with her in a fashion that made the boy cringe with concern. How could two people stand being so close? It was, to Manfred, as if their separate identities had flowed together, and the idea that such a muddling could be terrified him. (208–9)

The various motifs of the time-slips are present, to be sure (the horrible noise of the tape machine, Jack's closeness to Doreen), but it is as if the Manfred whose account we read here has no access to the consciousness of the Manfred who may or may not have been responsible for the awful cold squishy tendrils of subjectivity (conscious or unconscious) to which readers of—and characters in—*Martian Time-Slip* have just been subjected. This is just a frightened kid, apparently totally unaware that he is capable of warping everyone else's sense of time and space. But then again, maybe Arnie Kott, or Doreen, or somebody knows something about Manfred that Manfred himself does not and cannot know?

Yet even as Arnie tosses out his ambitious and plausible theory that Manfred controls time and "fooled around with last night" (I do love that phrase, and like to think of it applied to Benjy, who obviously fooled around with April 7, 1928), he sees in it nothing more than the potential to go back in time a couple of weeks and usurp Leo Bohlen's claim to the F.D.R. Mountains. (He eventually does this with the help of Manfred and an ancient Bleekman, and I will get back to this, too.) The desire is all the more repugnant inasmuch as it persists even after Helio has explained to Arnie the nature of Manfred's perception of time:

"This boy experiences his own old age, his lying in a dilapidated state, decades from now, in an old persons' home which is yet to be built here on Mars, a place of decay which he loathes beyond expression. In this future place he passes empty, weary years, bedridden—an object, not a person, kept alive through stupid legalities. When he tries to fix his eyes on the present, he almost at once is smitten by that dread vision of himself once again."

"Tell me about this old persons' home," Arnie said.

"It is to be built soon," Helio said. "Not for that purpose, but as a vast dormitory for immigrants to Mars."

"Yeah," Arnie said, recognizing it. "In the F.D.R. range."

"The people arrive," Helio said, "and settle, and live, and drive the wild Bleekmen from their last refuge. In turn, the Bleekmen put a curse on the land, sterile as it is. The Earth settlers fail; their buildings deteriorate year after year. Settlers return to Earth faster than they come here. At last this other use is made of the building: it becomes a home for the aged, for the poor, the senile and infirm." (226–27)

In other words, even after hearing all this—about the horror of Manfred's vision, the final dispossession of the Bleekmen, and the fate of the aged, poor, senile, and infirm on Mars—Arnie can still think only, *Yeah, yeah, and how can I get that land?*

You have probably intuited by now that there is not much to be gained in the critical observation that Arnie is a creep. But there is a more important structural point at stake here. Once one realizes that the time-slips are actually the key feature of the novel, and not just some weird textual juggling stunt that serves as a distraction from the main point (to put this another way, the novel is titled *Martian Time-Slip*, not *Martian Blockbuster Land Deal*), the entire novel starts to "leak" in the way Manfred's (un)consciousness does on that night, backwards and forwards from that sequence. On the most obvious thematic level, the novel reveals that it is primarily about schizophrenia, mental illness, and intellectual disability—situated on Mars, sure,

but a serious meditation on such matters nevertheless.[8] Diagnoses
and discussions of schizophrenia abound in the text; Jack tells an android teacher at the Public School (risibly named Kindly Dad) that
schizophrenia is "the most mysterious malady in all medicine" and
"it shows up in one out of every six people" (88), whereas his father,
Leo, reports that he heard on TV that the figure is "one in every three"
(133). During his visit to the Public School, Jack muses that autism is
defined as "a childhood form of schizophrenia, which a lot of people
had; schizophrenia was a major illness which touched sooner or later
almost every family" (73). At first autism is glossed as "oriented according to a subjective factor that took precedence over [a] sense of
objective reality" (72); one page later we read that "it meant, simply,
a person who could not live out the drives implanted in him by society" (73); four pages after that, "true autism, Jack had decided, was in
the last analysis an apathy toward public endeavor; it was a private
existence carried on as if the individual person were the creator of
all value, rather than merely the repository of inherited values" (77).

These definitions are not mutually exclusive, but they are not iden-
tical to each other, either; and for my purposes, the most important
thing about them is that there are so many of them. In Jack's many
ruminations on and memories of his own schizophrenic break, we
learn that Jack is especially (over)invested in the business of diagnosis, convinced as he is that "schizophrenia . . . is one of the most
pressing problems human civilization has ever faced" (88), "the most
pervasive, ominous psychic process known to man" (124–25). But he
is not alone: the psychiatrist Dr. Glaub reflects, in the course of his
attempts to diagnose Arnie Kott, that "often the first sign of the in-
sidious growth of the schizophrenic process in a person was an inability to eat in public" (110). More alarmingly, he reminds himself
that "generally, a concern with schizophrenia was a symptom of the
person's own inner struggle in that area" (110).

At this point, possibly, the novel has produced a perfect feedback loop in which the ratio of schizophrenics to the general population is not 1:6 or 1:3 but 1:1.[9] For every character in the book seems to have a concern with schizophrenia; even Heliogabalus, the Bleekman, has a theory. Declaring that "entire psychoanalysis is a vainglorious foolishness" (97), he proceeds to offer Arnie an indigenous Martian version of the 1960s countercultural, anti-psychiatry position on mental illness:

> "Purpose of life is unknown, and hence way to be is hidden from the eyes of living critters. Who can say if perhaps the schizophrenics are not correct? Mister, they take a brave journey. They turn away from mere things, which one may handle and turn to practical use; they turn inward to *meaning*. There, the black-night-without-bottom lies, the pit. Who can say if they will return? And if so, what will they be like, having glimpsed meaning? I admire them." (98)

Jack, by contrast, is horrified by thoughts like these: "*And people talk about mental illness as an escape!* He shuddered. It was no escape; it was a narrowing, a contracting of life into, at last, a moldering, dank tomb, a place where nothing came or went; a place of total death" (154). In his spells, Jack sees "through" people to the hidden cyborgs within, constructed of wire, plastic, and steel; Manfred sees a world of gubbish that degrades not only people and things but language itself, so that eventually the text itself becomes (in one of the time-slips) nothing more than "gubble, gubble gubble gubble, *gubble!*" (179). But the leakage does not stop here: once we understand the pervasiveness of schizophrenia and intellectual disability in the text, we can reread the novel's opening sentence as a time-slip take on a form of American suburban ennui that was just percolating to the surface in 1964: "From the depths of phenobarbital slumber, Silvia Bohlen heard something that called" (1). She rouses herself at 9:30, long after her son and husband have gotten up, and decides, "I must not take any more of that"—phenobarbital, one assumes—"better to succumb to the schizophrenic process, join the rest of the world" (1). So now, as we reread the text *as* a text about intellectual disability, we come to understand that the schizophrenic process isolates one from the rest of the world, inducing an apathy toward public endeavor and an inability to live out the drives implanted in us by society—and that, paradoxically, everybody else is in the same boat.

Leaving aside the pedestrian point that it was silly to imagine in 1964 that humans would have established colonies on Mars within thirty years (a minor point about Dick's liberties with verisimilitude, I think, in a fictional landscape in which Mars has air, water, arable land, giant insects, and Bleekmen), time seems weird throughout the book. The possibility that "time flowed differently on Earth than Mars" is introduced very early in the novel, and attributed to "an article in a psychology journal" (5). I have already remarked that although Mars is the future (as Anne Esterhazy puts it), it is already crumbling; by the same token, Earth artifacts are spoken of as if they are inconceivably ancient. At one point Arnie tells Heliogabalus that he has "a long-playing record . . . so goddamn old and valuable that I don't dare play it. . . . Glenn Gould playing. It's forty years old; my family passed it down to me" (95). The Bleekmen confuse matters still further. Jack imagines—with good reason, it turns out—that Manfred would do better living with them ("possibly their sense of time is close to his" [150]), and toward the end of the novel, as Arnie prepares to go back in time to stake his claim to the F.D.R. Mountains, Heliogabalus informs him that he must go with Manfred to the Bleekmen's sacred rock, Dirty Knobby, for even though "the rock alone is powerless," Manfred's presence will enable Arnie's time travel because "time is weakest at that spot where Dirty Knobby lies" (236).

On one reading, then, the novel's real estate plot (to abuse the pun) seems to be supplanted by the formal experiment of the time-slips and their resonance for the rest of the book: the former is merely the vehicle for the latter, just as Pynchon's *Crying of Lot 49*, a book similarly predicated on real estate and plotting, reveals itself ultimately to be a text about the possibility of a network of secret societies communicating by an alternative mail system. I have suggested as much to students, arguing (plausibly, to gauge by their responses) that none of them winds up reading the book for an answer to the question, *Will Arnie succeed in staking his claim?* And yet the real estate plot and the time-slips are more complexly interwoven, such that the latter do not supplant the former so much as infect it. Arnie does succeed in going back in time, but his time travel is Manfredized, so that even though the book begins to re-narrate its second chapter as Arnie starts his workday, the machinery starts to break down, and even Arnie's copy of the *New York Times* begins to read, "gubble gubble" (254).

More alarmingly, the novel then proceeds to replay the scene in which we first met the Bleekmen, back in chapter 2; Jack Bohlen stops his helicopter to offer water to some dying nomads (refusal to do so is a violation of U.N. law), whereas Arnie, traveling in his own helicopter, balks at doing so. In gratitude, the Bleekmen give Jack a charm, a "water witch"; they tell him, "It will bring you water, the source of life, any time you need" (31), and later, conversing with Arnie, Heliogabalus claims that "it may guarantee him safety" if anyone tries to harm Jack. Now, I believe it was Chekhov who once said that if you introduce a mysterious supernatural device into your text in chapter 2, it has to be used in chapter 16. In the time-travel replay of the water witch scene, Arnie tries to kill Jack, and is shot with a poisoned arrow by the Bleekmen. Can Arnie die in the past? Can he already have died? Is it like dying in a dream? And is this his dream, or Manfred's? As Arnie ponders these questions, he stumbles onto the possibility that the time-slips in the novel began not when Manfred was introduced to the text, but when the Bleekmen brought out the water witch:

> How did that young Bleekman catch on so fast? They don't ordinarily use their arrows on Earth people; it's a capital crime. It means the end of them.
>
> Maybe, he thought, they were expecting me. They conspired to save Bohlen because he gave them food and water. Arnie thought, I bet they're the ones who gave him the water witch. Of course. *And when they gave it to him they knew. They knew about all this, even back then, at the very beginning.* (264; emphasis in original)

There is some serious verb-tense confusion going on here. How can it be that the Bleekmen conspired, in the past, to save Bohlen from Arnie's murderous attack weeks later? Arnie's hypothesis is that the Bleekmen, like Manfred, can come unstuck in time, and prophetically see in their first encounter with him the as-yet-unrealized time-travel version of the repetition of their encounter with him. What is the tense in which Arnie's realization can be expressed? *Now I know that in the past, the Bleekmen will have conspired to revisit the moment that was the present at the time I met them, and its repetition in the future, which is now the present from which I have traveled back to this moment in the past (as they knew I would do)?*

For the record, Arnie does eventually return to "real" time, whatever that might mean by now, where he is killed by a business rival (though he believes he is still in an altered time-travel state in which he cannot die). And Manfred escapes the fate of AM-WEB, living with the Bleekmen for the remainder of his days and returning in the novel's enigmatic final scene at the end of this climactic day, now a very old man visiting from the future, to thank Jack for trying to help him long ago. "It wasn't long ago," Jack replies. "Have you forgotten? You came back to us; it was just today. This is your distant past, when you were a boy" (277). (Again, the verb tense is inscrutable: one wonders what "have you forgotten" can possibly mean here.) It is not entirely a happy ending; elderly Manfred is very much the tubes-and-wires, "pumps and hoses and dials" (276) cyborg he feared becoming. But he escaped AM-WEB, and that, it turns out, was the point; that, finally, is why he (and the Bleekmen?) fooled around with the temporal fabric of the novel.

The mystical link between Manfred and the Bleekmen is a bit embarrassing, politically; Helio explains that he can communicate with the boy because "we are both prisoners, Mister, in a hostile land" (226), as if they are speaking by way of a special Subaltern Subchannel. Helio thereby becomes a version of what is known among film critics as the "magic Negro" who, according to Todd Boyd, is given "special powers and underlying mysticism."[10] But the Subaltern Subchannel, for all its orientalizing faults, helps to clarify the link between AM-WEB and Camp Ben-Gurion, which is never made explicit until Helio offers Arnie that extended exposition of Manfred's deepest fears. Let us now return to Camp Ben-Gurion—or, more precisely, to Norbert Steiner's visit to see his son, which almost immediately convinces him to kill himself. After shocking the Camp B-G staff by declaring that he believes the facility *should* be shut down, on the grounds that his son "will never be able to hold a job. . . . He'll always be a burden on society, like he is now" (44), Norbert stops by the Red Fox restaurant and gets an earful of even more vicious eugenics discourse from the owner:

"Why you looking so glum, Norb?"
Steiner said, "They're going to close down Camp B-G."

"Good," the owner of the Red Fox said. "We don't need those freaks here on Mars; it's bad advertising."

"I agree," Steiner said, "at least to a certain extent."

"It's like those babies with seal flippers back in the '60s, from them using that German drug. They should have destroyed all of them; there's plenty of healthy normal children born, why spare those others? If you had a kid with extra arms or no arms, deformed in some way, you wouldn't want it kept alive, would you?"

"No," Steiner said. He did not say that his wife's brother back on Earth was a phocomelus; he had been born without arms and made use of superb artificial ones designed for him by a Canadian firm which specialized in such equipment. (49)

The plot thickens, as if it weren't already thick enough: writing in the wake of the controversy over Thalidomide (that German drug, first marketed in 1957 by Chemie Grünenthal), Dick suggests that the genocidal impulse toward people with disabilities will survive well into the future, even though Steiner's brother-in-law appears to have himself some pretty fabulous prostheses (and no intellectual disabilities).

Last but certainly not least, Arnie Kott himself has a child in Camp B-G, a child he fathered with Anne Esterhazy; damaged by exposure to gamma rays in utero, the child is three years old, "small and shriveled, with enormous eyes like a lemur's . . . [and] peculiar webbed fingers" (40). Arnie's attitude toward the child is predictable: close the camp and kill the kids.

"I've been sorry ever since those Jews opened that camp."

Anne said, "Bless you, honest blunt Arnie Kott, mankind's best friend."

"It tells the entire world we've got nuts here on Mars, that if you travel across space to get here you're apt to damage your sexual organs and give birth to a monster that would make those German flipper-people look like your next-door neighbor."

"You and the gentleman who runs the Red Fox."

"I'm just being hard-headedly realistic. We're in a struggle for our life; we've got to keep people emigrating here or we're dead on the vine, Annie. You know that. If we didn't have Camp B-G we could advertise that away from Earth's H-bomb-testing, contaminated atmosphere there are no abnormal births. I hope to see that, but Camp B-G spoils it."

"Not Camp B-G. The births themselves."

"No one would be able to check up and show our abnormal births," Arnie said, "without B-G." (64–65)

The realm of biopower, apparently, does not quite extend (yet) to Mars, where the sciences of population management are weaker than they are on Earth and no one will know about disability if Camp B-G is shut down—and where Arnie is apparently unaware that back on Earth, some of those German flipper-people *are* your next-door neighbors, outfitted with superb artificial limbs. And as it happens, the U.N.'s thinking is not very far from Arnie's; indeed, it is later in this very conversation with his ex-wife (though oddly, this part of the exchange is not narrated directly, but merely recalled by Arnie in the following chapter) that Arnie learns of the U.N.'s plan to develop land in the F.D.R. mountain range. He had already heard that someone was interested in the land; Anne happens to know of various rumors, one of which is that the U.N. "intended to build an enormous supranational park, a sort of Garden of Eden, to lure emigrants out of Earth" (94). The insinuation here, then, is that the building of AM-WEB (the Garden of Eden reimagined as an enormous supranational park on Mars?) and the closing of Camp Ben-Gurion are two facets of the same plan: lure emigrants from Earth, and suppress all official acknowledgment of the existence of people with disabilities on Mars. Manfred's vision of his cyborg future is thus also a vision of imminent genocide.

Martian Time-Slip represents one of Anglophone literature's most fascinating attempts to textualize intellectual disability. By this I mean that the novel is not merely *about* disability; that much should be clear as plastic by now. If The Sound and the Fury is (among other things) a register of the fate of the "feebleminded" in the 1920s, Martian Time-Slip is (among other things) a response to the discourse of eliminationism, in which the United Nations turns out to be the exterminator-in-general and only the Israeli encampment on Mars has learned the lessons of recent history well enough to provide shelter and care for children like Manfred Steiner. But Martian Time-Slip is also very much more than that: it is a stunning example of how, in Quayson's terms, the dominant protocols of representation within the literary text are short-circuited in relation to disability. Admittedly, for some readers, the radical experimentalism of Martian Time-Slip can be explained away by the very fact that it belongs to the genre of science fiction, where writers are permitted to concoct outlandish things like time travel and extraterrestrial civilizations, and where the dominant protocols of representation tend to defy the dominant protocols of representation in mainstream fiction on a page-by-page basis. But I think the objection only strengthens my point. This convoluted narrative experiment set on a ridiculously implausible Mars nevertheless provides a vehicle for a profound deliberation on time, space, mental illness, and intellectual disability. And as in The Sound and the Fury, it is critical that the disability chronotope is predicated on an unambiguously *fictional* disability—and yet poses the question, in the starkest of terms, of how to treat the most vulnerable humans among us.

* * *

And yet when it comes to vulnerability, humans are not the only creatures worth attending to. I remarked earlier that the disability chronotope can offer an outlet into realms of temporal experience that exceed human perception. In *Martian Time-Slip*, Manfred's fictional disability opens onto time scales that (presumably) only the Bleekmen can comprehend; but critically, it also offers a link to the nonhuman. Our very first encounter with Manfred's free indirect discourse arrives without warning after a brief break in the text, and without any warning that it is Manfred's free indirect discourse, like so:

> High in the sky circled meat-eating birds. At the base of the windowed building lay their excrement. He picked up the wads until he held several. They twisted and turned like dough, and he knew there were living creatures within; he carried them carefully into the open corridor of the building. One wad opened, parted with a split in its woven, hairlike side; it became too large to hold, and he saw it now in the wall. A compartment where it lay on its side, the rent so wide that he perceived the creature within.
>
> Gubbish! A worm, coiled up, made of wet, bony-white pleats, the inside gubbish worm, from a person's body. If only the high-flying birds could find it and eat it down, like that. He ran down the steps, which gave beneath his feet. Boards missing. He saw down through the sieve of wood to the soil beneath, the cavity, dark, cold, full of wood so rotten that it lay in damp powder, destroyed by gubbish-rot.
>
> Arms lifted up, tossed him to the circling birds; he floated up, falling at the same time. They ate his head off. And then he stood on a bridge over the sea. Sharks showed in the water, their sharp, cutting fins. He caught one on his line and it came sliding up from the water,

mouth open, to swallow him. He stepped back, but the bridge caved in and sagged so that the water reached his middle.

It rained gubbish, now; all was gubbish, wherever he looked. A group of those who didn't like him appeared at the end of the bridge and held up a loop of shark teeth. He was emperor. They crowned him with the loop, and he tried to thank them. But they forced the loop down past his head to his neck, and they began to strangle him. They knotted the loop and the shark teeth cut his head off. Once more he sat in the dark, damp basement with the powdery rot around him, listening to the tidal water lap-lapping everywhere. A world where gubbish ruled, and he had no voice; the shark teeth had cut his voice out.

I am Manfred, he said. (137–38)

Again, this may not seem terribly out of line in a work of science fiction, where the parameters of mimesis are potentially infinite. You might even decide that this is little more than literary gubbish. But then compare it to this passage in a National Book Award-winning work of mainstream fiction, which appears without warning early in a narrative that, up to this point, has faithfully adhered to the dominant protocols of realistic representation:

A flock of birds, each one burning. Stars swoop down to bullets. Hot red specks take flesh, nest there, a body part, part body. Lasts forever: no change to measure. Flock of fiery cinders. When grey pain of them thins, then always water. Flattest width so slow it fails as liquid. Nothing in the end but flow. Nextless stream, lowest thing above knowing. A thing itself the cold and so can't feel it. (10)

This is from Richard Powers's 2006 novel *The Echo Maker*, and the passage might—one cannot say for certain—be focalized through a young man named Mark Schluter, who has sustained a devastating brain injury as the result of a mysterious accident in which his truck careened off an empty road at eighty miles per hour at 2:00 a.m. As Mark gradually regains consciousness, and as he slowly reacquires the ability to speak, we learn that he has suffered a rare neurological disorder known as Capgras syndrome. People with Capgras syndrome are unable to recognize their loved ones as their loved ones; they recognize the faces of their family members, but they do not recognize them as their family members. (In neurological terms, the amygdala and the inferotemporal cortex have somehow become disconnected: the facial recognition systems of the brain are working, but have lost their connection to the emotional-processing centers that would make sense of those recognitions.) In their attempt to make sense of the fact that they recognize deeply familiar faces but have no emotional attachment to them, they come to believe that their family members have been replaced by doubles, androids, or impersonators. It is a devastating disorder, and some people with Capgras have snapped completely: as Powers writes, "a young Capgras sufferer from the British Midlands, to prove that his father was a robot, had cut the man open to expose the wires" (89–90).

It sounds like material for Oliver Sacks, and, indeed, half of the novel is devoted to an Oliver Sacks–like character named Gerald Weber, to whom Mark Schluter's sister, Karin, writes in despair. Weber's growing self-doubt and eventual breakdown make up one strand of the plot; another involves water use, ecotourism, real estate development (this time on Earth), and the migration patterns of sandhill cranes, who stop every year in the Schluters' hometown of Kearney, Nebraska. Most important for our purposes, the novel speculates repeatedly about the mental capacities of birds: "Birds will surprise you," says Karin's boyfriend, the conservationist Daniel Riegel. "Blue jays can lie. Ravens punish social cheaters. Crows fashion hooks out of straight wire and use them to lift cups out of holes. Not even chimps can do that" (388). "What does it feel like, to be a bird?" the novel asks (424), renewing Thomas Nagel's question about bats. Karin Schluter is led to an epiphany about her own species:

> The whole race suffered from Capgras. Those birds danced like our next of kin, looked like our next of kin, called and willed and parented and taught and navigated all just like our blood relations. Half their parts were still ours. Yet humans waved them off: impostors. At most, a strange spectacle to gaze at from a blind. (348)

That epiphany is central to the novel as a whole; one might even say that it constitutes the message that Powers might have sent via Western Union. *These birds are our next of kin.* The boondoggle real estate deal (here on Earth, not on Mars) that will create a wildlife habitat preserve in Kearney is nothing more than a scam that will lead to, at most, a way to gaze at the strange spectacle of the cranes from a blind.

It is possible, then, that the "flock of birds, each one burning" passage is narrated from the perspective of the sandhill cranes themselves, and is not Mark Schluter's postinjury interior monologue. Perhaps "nextless stream, lowest thing above knowing" is what cranes "think" as they soar over the prairie. Yet we are tempted to "humanize" those narrative interludes not only because we continue to believe that humans are the only creatures capable of narrative but also because the interludes seem to "progress" into increasing intelligibility: the second such interlude, for instance, begins,

> Rises up in flooded fields. There is a wave, a rocking in the reeds. Pain again, then nothing. When sense returns, he is drowning. Father teaching him to swim. Current in his limbs. Four years old, and his father floating him. Flying, then flailing, then falling. His father grabbing his leg, pulling him under. (18–19)

These seem to be the sense impressions of a human being, a human being who has or had a father teaching him to swim when he was four. But it is many pages before Mark's narrative interludes can rejoin the fabric of the main narrative. Until then, the plot of *The Echo Maker* turns on the question of whether Mark Schluter himself will come to understand the plot—not the plot he thinks has been hatched against him, which (he believes) eventually includes his sister, his dog, his house, and the town of Kearney (all of which have been overtaken by impostors), but the plot of the novel we are reading. Narratively, Powers is working with a variation of what we might call the Flowers for Algernon Protocol, whereby shades and degrees of mental impairment are registered on the page by a character's capacity for narrative.

But perhaps the surprise and disorientation of the first "flock of birds" passage lingers, and the suggestion hovers over the remainder of the novel—that we need to be able to see with birds' eyes, think with (what we imagine to be) bird brains, in order to understand adequately the ecosystem we are destroying. As in *Martian Time-Slip*, the experimental narrative technique opens out onto a principle of great breadth: the discourse of "sustainability," and even the discourse of the Anthropocene, are still all about *us*. The former foregrounds our needs as a species, asking us to ease off the throttle of postindustrial plunder a bit so that we can sustain our resources and our way of life; the latter puts us firmly in the center of geological change, environmental devastation, and mass extinctions. The discourse of the Anthropocene offers a conceptual advance over the discourse of "sustainability" insofar as it calls for a realization more radical than that which will produce a kinder, gentler form of resource extraction for human consumption; more important for our understanding of temporality in this study, it compels us to look beyond human time scales into the abyss—and into a consciousness that can think, "lasts forever: no change to measure."[11]

The question of the grounds for designating an "Anthropocene epoch" and the implications of this designation for the humanities are matters beyond the scope of this book, but I hope I can sketch out an argument for why such things are important to an understanding of intellectual disability and narrative.[12] In *Reading for the Plot*, Peter Brooks writes that two of the five modes elaborated in Barthes's *S/Z* are critical to the temporal structure of plot: "Plot, then, might best be thought of as an 'overcoding' of the proairetic by the hermeneutic"—that is, the mode of action by the mode of enigma— "the latter structuring the discrete elements of the former into larger interpretive wholes, working out their play of meaning and significance" (18). For those of you who are not steeped in narrative theory, let me paraphrase this.[13] Barthes's "proairetic" code covers the events of a narrative: this happened, this happened, this happened. The "hermeneutic" code bestows significance on them: this happened for that reason, this character took away such and such an understanding from that encounter. For Brooks, then, "plot" is an operation by which a narrative presents the question, "What things are we reading about?" and supplements it with, "So why are we reading about them anyway?" This is an elemental operation, to be sure, the kind of thing that might lead one's children to say, "That's not a story" when one offers them a series of colors or objects. In *Martian Time-Slip*, Manfred's function is to disrupt the overcoding of the proairetic by the hermeneutic, to throw awry and to rewrite the frame by which the actions of the narrative are to be understood.

Ricoeur says something similar about the narrative function of Septimus Warren Smith in *Mrs. Dalloway*, suggesting that he becomes a vehicle for shuttling between mortal time and monumental time: "In his madness, Septimus is the bearer of a revelation that grasps in time the obstacle to a vision of cosmic unity and in death the way of reaching this salvific meaning" (1985, 103). Monumental time, for Ricoeur, is still a form of human time, not the time sounded throughout the novel by Big Ben but (from Nietzsche) "the time of authority-figures" (1985, 106). It is what permits Septimus to have a vision of Evans, his dead comrade from the Great War; and it is occasioned, appropriately, by the very word "time," spoken by his wife. The revelation is only slightly less strange than anything one might find in *Martian Time-Slip*:

> "It is time," said Rezia.
>
> The word "time" split its husk; poured its riches over him; and from his lips fell like shells, like shavings from a plane, without his making them, hard, white, imperishable words, and flew to attach themselves to their places in an ode to Time; an immortal ode to Time. He sang. Evans answered from behind the tree. The dead were in Thessaly, Evans sang, among the orchids. There they waited till the War was over, and now the dead, now Evans himself—
>
> "For God's sake don't come!" Septimus cried out. For he could not look upon the dead.
>
> But the branches parted. A man in grey was actually walking towards them. It was Evans! But no mud was on him; no wounds; he was not changed. I must tell the whole world, Septimus cried, raising his hand (as the dead man in the grey suit came nearer), raising his hand like some colossal figure who has lamented the fate of man for ages in the desert alone with his hands pressed to his forehead, furrows of despair on his cheeks, and now sees light on the desert's edge which broadens and strikes the iron-black figure. (68)

For Ricoeur, the eerie connection between Septimus and his "double," Clarissa Dalloway, makes it imperative that "we must . . . never lose sight of the fact that what makes sense is the juxtaposition of Septimus's and Clarissa's experience of time" (1985, 109), such that

Septimus's suicide somehow allows Mrs. Dalloway to go on living: "If Septimus's refusal of monumental time was able to direct Mrs. Dalloway back toward transitory life and its precarious joys, this is because it set her on the path to a mortal time that is fully assumed" (190). The brief passage in *Mrs. Dalloway* that is centered on the beggar woman, the "rusty pump," goes still further, giving us access to planetary time on Powers's scale: "Through all ages—when the pavement was grass, when it was swamp, through the age of tusk and mammoth, through the age of silent sunrise . . . this battered old woman . . . would still be there in ten million years" (79–80). This is "the voice of an ancient spring spouting from the earth" (79), we are told, though because her song consists of "ee um fah um so / fee swee too ccm oo," it is not clear that perception of time on this scale, in Woolf's radical version of intellectually disabled narrative, is even remotely intelligible to us.

And there is so much that is unintelligible to us, is there not? Time, space, life—and the enduring question of why there is something rather than nothing. (Spoiler alert: this book will not attempt to answer that question.) I want to close by suggesting that *The Sound and the Fury* offers a different kind of intellectual disability chronotope that opens out onto the unintelligible. This claim is at once less and more risky than my claims about *Martian Time-Slip*, *The Echo Maker*, and *Mrs. Dalloway*. Less, because Faulkner's form of the unintelligible is mediated by Christianity, and is therefore (to adapt and abuse Donald Rumsfeld's most oft-cited sentence) an intelligible unintelligible. More, because there is no way for me to argue decisively than Benjy's narrative is the device that gets us there. The revelation—and I use the word advisedly—is Dilsey's, and it is induced by the Reverend Shegog's Easter sermon, not by her metafictional reading of the first section of the book in which she appears. Nevertheless, she attends Easter service with Benjy, fending off Frony's complaint that "folks talkin" about his presence in the church with the thoroughly Christian rebuttal, "Tell um de good Lawd dont keer whether he bright or not. Dont nobody but white trash keer dat" (290). And if Benjy is the holy innocent throughout (a big "if," I grant), then it may be of some moment that Dilsey is his companion throughout the climactic sermon: "In the midst of the voices and the hands Ben sat, rapt in his sweet blue gaze. Dilsey sat bolt upright beside, crying rigidly and quietly in the annealment and the blood of the remembered Lamb" (297).

The revelation is nothing less than Dilsey's sense of an ending: she has been vouchsafed the insight that Frank Kermode contends is the purpose of narrative. In the middle of the journey of her life—or, to be more precise, somewhere near its final stages—she finds herself in a dark wood, until she sees, at Reverend Shegog's urging, "de resurrection en de light" (297). Censorious yet again, Frony asks her to stop crying on the way home, because "we be passin white folks soon"; Dilsey responds in such a way as to let us know that she has been given access to the unintelligible.

> "I've seed de first en de last," Dilsey said. "Never you mind me."
>
> "First en last whut?" Frony said.
>
> "Never you mind," Dilsey said. "I seed de beginnin, en now I sees de endin." (297)

This certainly sounds like a vision of sacred time, but we still need to ask Frony's question: the first and last *what*, exactly? (And why should it involve Benjy?)[14] Dilsey sees the beginning and the ending of the Compsons' decline, perhaps. The beginning and the ending of her own life. The beginning and the ending of the life of Christ. Perhaps the beginning and ending of it all, from Genesis to Revelation; or, more modestly but no less profoundly, the beginning and the ending of the narrative she inhabits.

Though this may sound ridiculously metafictional to some readers, equating an understanding of the unfolding of God's plan for salvation with an understanding of the novel in which one is a character, I am not trying to trivialize Dilsey's moment of illumination. On the contrary, I consider it to be the real "conclusion" to the novel—even as I hedge this "conclusion" in scare quotes, for I am aware that there is another, plasterboard conclusion in the novel's final pages, whereby Benjy is mollified when Jason violently takes control of the carriage, swings the horse to the right of the monument, and restores Benjy's sense of order "as each cornice and façade flowed smoothly once more from left to right, post and tree, window and doorway and signboard each in its ordered place" (321). That plasterboard conclusion, this Potemkin-village understanding of order as Benjy (apparently) perceives it, quite clearly threatens to torpedo any argument that Benjy's intellectually disabled understanding of the world can become the vehicle for Dilsey's cosmic sense of revelation. But that is precisely the challenge with which Faulkner has confronted us by offering two endings in his novel about beginnings and endings.[15] And I submit that even if Dilsey is merely gifted with a vision of the novel in which she is a character, it is no small accomplishment to comprehend the narrative you inhabit.

For the mechanics of what Kermode called "tick-tock" narratives, fictions with intelligible beginnings and ends, presume that "all such plotting presupposes that an end will bestow upon the whole duration and meaning" (46). And Dilsey emphatically achieves that end; to suggest that *The Sound and the Fury* does not, to remark that it does not rest content in telling us that we must have the recollection and the blood of the Lamb in order to see the beginning and the ending, is simply to acknowledge that *The Sound and the Fury* is a modern novel, and that, as Kermode allows, "our skepticism, our changed principles of reality, force us to discard the fictions that are too fully explanatory, too consoling" (161). Dilsey's sense of divine narrative order is therefore juxtaposed and contrasted with, but not ultimately undermined by, the far weaker and more ephemeral order announced on its final page. Contrast Dilsey's sense of completion with that of Michael K, where the deployment of intellectual disability works to a drastically different end. I remarked in the previous chapter that *Life and Times of Michael K* poses substantial problems for narrative theory, insofar as so much of it does not appear to be a story at all. Here I want to focus on the concluding paragraph, in which Michael K is imagining a journey with an old man who is looking at a well destroyed by soldiers and worrying about where he will get water:

> He, Michael K, would produce a teaspoon from his pocket, a teaspoon and a long roll of string. He would clear the rubble from the mouth of the shaft, he would bend the handle of the teaspoon in a loop and tie the string to it, he would lower it down the shaft deep into the earth, and when he brought it up there would be water in the bowl of the spoon; and in that way, he would say, one can live. (183–84)

Whatever one makes of Michael K's status as *Homo sacer* supercrip, this is a deliberately anticlimactic ending, appropriate to a novel that, as we have seen, does not have much of a plot. Compared with this radical *diminuendo*, even the final page of *The Sound and the Fury* sounds like a rousing climax; if Michael K's intellectual disability provides *Michael K* with much of its motive, it also renders his life and times as a narrative of "tick-tick-tick" rather than "tick-tock,"[16] producing an ending starkly devoid of any sense of duration or meaning—just a teaspoon of water, and a hypothetical one at that.

Moreover, the point needs to be made (and so I will make it) that *The Sound and the Fury* offers a model for Dilsey's vision of totality, and it consists precisely of Benjy's existence beyond temporality: it sees the first and the last, the beginning and the ending. Granted,

Benjy's section is not a literary version of Augustine's vision of God's existence beyond temporality—partly because Benjy is not God, partly because Augustine's understanding of eternity pointedly excludes temporality (since God created time), and partly because Benjy does not seem to have any way of apprehending and narrating the events of his world after April 7, 1928 (as Augustine notes, any comprehensive sense of time would have to account for the phenomenon of prophecy). But for the purposes of my argument, it does not matter whether Benjy is conscious of his narrative dynamics, or whether Dilsey is aware of them. It does not matter that Benjy's narrative is structured as tick-tick-tick, opening with golf (and a sense of loss) and closing with the dark flowing in "smooth, bright shapes" (and drifting off to sleep as a young child, held by Caddy, who is thereby restored to Benjy's side). It matters only that Benjy's section exists as a synoptic mode of apprehending time in a narrative one of whose characters has a revelation about seeing the beginning and the ending. Only in this sense can we speak of Benjy as the vehicle for Dilsey's revelation. Manfred Steiner's leap beyond human time is a more secular version of the intellectual disability chronotope, revealing the evanescence and futility of our getting and spending (which lay waste Arnie Kott's powers); whereas for Dilsey, nothing matters but the recollection and the blood of the Lamb. And even if we secular modern readers, unconsoled by endings that are too explanatory, are uninterested in the question of what will happen to our immortal souls (particularly if we do not believe we possess them), there yet remains another crucial question, that of how we are to treat the Benjys and the Manfreds and the Septimuses and beggar women among us, regardless of whether we can understand them.

My only caveat about this reading of Dilsey, narrative temporality, and intellectual disability is that it once again gives us a version of the magical Negro who occupies the space (and time) of transition

between the intelligible and the unintelligible world. Dilsey and Heliogabalus: quasi-miraculous agents of ambiguous salvation. This is
an unfortunately seductive tableau for white American writers, even
white American writers so unlike each other as William Faulkner and
Philip K. Dick; and it raises the broader question of how we are to
understand historical and national variations on the intellectual disability chronotope. For the rendering of characters with intellectual
disabilities has significant implications for American literature even
though no intellectual disability is specifically American. The United
States has the dubious distinction of being the nation that took the
premises of late nineteenth-century eugenics, developed in England
by Francis Galton, and turned them into an industry whose purpose
it was to identify the (often textual) markers of intellectual disability.
Likewise, it was a series of American researchers—H. H. Goddard,
Lewis Terman, and R. M. Yerkes—who took Alfred Binet's intelligence test and converted it from a device meant to identify children
who might need extra assistance in learning to a device for ranking
humans and reifying a narrow and scientifically unsound idea of
heritable intelligence (see Gould 176–234). That project was fueled
by white Americans' profound anxieties about race and immigration,
and provided pseudoscientific justification for the severe inequities
of industrial capitalism; it led not only to the displays of "good" and
"bad" families in textbooks and state fairs but also to the practices
of institutionalization and involuntary sterilization, which affected
people with a wide variety of conditions from Down syndrome to ep-
ilepsy. A specter haunted the American century, one might say—the
specter of intellectual disability.[17] It is all the more urgently important, then—not in spite of these ideological limitations but precisely
because of them—to find in fictional modes of intellectual disability
a way of imagining other ways of being human that expose and tran-
scend the limitations of our own space and time.

CHAPTER THREE

Self-Awareness

Literary texts have any number of ways of marking their awareness of themselves as literary texts. Some are cloying; some are trivial; some are merely cute. Some involve explicitly metafictional engagements with the fictionality of fiction, as in the closing passage of Beckett's *Molloy*, echoing and complicating the opening passage of the novella's second section: "Then I went back into the house and wrote, It is midnight. The rain is beating on the windows. It was not midnight. It was not raining" (176). Some involve more subtle, implicit meditations on the degree of readerly self-consciousness necessary for reading, as in Pynchon's *Crying of Lot 49*, where Oedipa is likened to Maxwell's Demon, sorting through information as she makes her way through the text, or as in Arthur Conan Doyle's story "The Naval Treaty," in which Holmes explains that the difficulty of the case stemmed from its surfeit of evidence, so that the detective had to serve as a kind of information-sorting demon: "What was vital was overlaid and hidden by what was irrelevant. Of all the facts which were presented to us we had to pick just those which we deemed to be essential, and then piece them together in their order so as to reconstruct this very remarkable chain of events" (467–68). Of this passage

Peter Brooks writes, "Here we have a clear *ars poetica*, of the detective and the novelist, and of the plotting of the narrative as an example of the mental operation described by Wallace Stevens as 'The poem of the mind in the act of finding / What will suffice'" (29). If indeed Brooks is right, and I believe he is, then all detective fiction serves in one way or another as an implicit commentary on the operations of reading fiction; and if we introduce into a detective fiction a detective with an intellectual disability that serves him well, like the obsessive-compulsive Adrian Monk (the central figure of USA Network's *Monk*, the acclaimed series that ran from 2002 to 2009), then we confront the intriguing possibility that for some implicit meditations on the operations of reading fiction, certain kinds of intellectual disability render one a more capable reader of certain genres of fiction. The dynamic is especially lively in detective fiction, since detective fiction is almost always recursive, rewarding those characters in the narrative who are the most capable readers of detective fiction.

This is a possibility to which I will return in discussing *The Curious Incident of the Dog in the Night-Time*, which is, among other things, a metafictional commentary on the implicitly metafictional nature of detective fiction, and on (obviously) the relation of intellectual disability to narrative; for now, to broaden the terrain before us, I'd like to start this chapter by returning to the genre of young adult fiction—this time, the first installment of Philip Pullman's *His Dark Materials* series, *The Golden Compass*. The passage is focalized through Pullman's heroine, eleven-year-old Lyra Belacqua:

> With every second that went past, with every sentence she spoke, she felt a little strength flowing back. And now that she was doing something difficult and familiar and never quite predictable, namely, lying, she felt a sort of mastery again, the same sense of complexity and control that the alethiometer gave her. She had to be careful not to say

anything obviously impossible; she had to be vague in some places and invent plausible details in others; she had to be an artist, in short. (246)

I call attention to this passage partly because it provides readers with a young-adult version of Odysseus—Lyra is a character whose talent for fabulation matches, and in a way inspires, the narrative she inhabits—and partly because Pullman is so clearly messing with us here. Let us review: Lyra has to be careful not to say anything obviously impossible; she needs to mix vagueness with plausibility. She has to be a realist narrator, within her fictional frame of reference. Readers familiar with the *His Dark Materials* trilogy will know that Pullman draws on the "multiple universes" hypothesis, in which an infinite series of possible universes inhabits the very fabric of space-time, in order to set his Lyra on an Earth very like our own, where Lyra can gambol and frolic about the colleges of Oxford, except for the fact that in Lyra's Earth, the Reformation never happened; the Republic of Texas is a sovereign nation; zeppelins constitute the most technologically advanced means of transport; and the landscape is populated by witches, talking armored bears, and the animal "daemons" who are the literal embodiment of each human being's soul. As you may have gathered from the excerpt quoted above, Lyra's universe also includes a device called an "alethiometer," a kind of Heideggerian compass that discloses the truth, which Lyra is particularly adept at reading. You could say that Pullman has a lot of cheek, cautioning his heroine against saying anything obviously impossible in a world of wildly speculative fiction. But then, you could say that Pullman is being an artist, in short.

But Lyra, like Odysseus, is a very clever character. One gets the sense, in her epic journey and in his, that either of them could seize control of the narrative on the grounds that *they* are the most inventive and capable storytellers around: indeed, since much of Homer's and Pullman's task consists of conveying their brilliant, fanciful, yet ultimately plausible lies to us, why don't we just cut out the middleman and listen to Odysseus and Lyra directly? It is a preposterous question: these are not real people. They never existed, except on the page. Their cleverness is but an artifact of the cleverness of their creators; they are surrogates for their creators, just as detectives are surrogates for both authors and readers in their genre. But what are they doing in, or to, their narratives?

Perhaps they are there to instruct and delight. Or, to take the more recent answer offered by Lisa Zunshine in *Why We Read Fiction*, they are there to engage our ability to entertain the possibility that other people might have false beliefs, and our ability to imagine that other people might be lying. I'll get back to Zunshine's work later in this chapter, but for now I simply want to put forward the fairly uncontroversial proposition that it can indeed be delightful and instructive to watch a good liar at work, and that fictional texts have been making use of this insight from *The Odyssey* to *The Confidence-Man* to *Dirty Rotten Scoundrels* and *House of Games*. There is much to be gained, cognitively, from inhabiting or intuiting the minds of Odysseus and Lyra Belacqua, and perhaps the delight is all the greater for the possibility of contemplating their relation to the fictional universes they inhabit, which are full of weird things you don't see every day, like one-eyed giants and enchantresses and daemons and talking armored bears. But as every competent reader knows, those weird things are indices that we *are* in fictional worlds; they serve as reminders that we are reading fiction and not history, even though the Trojan War really happened and the hypothesis of multiple universes is as plausible as anything else in the wacky world of cosmology and astrophysics. In Zunshine's terms, these textual oddities allow our metarepresentational capacities to supply the narrative with a "source tag" whereby we attribute the narrative to a source (Homer, Philip Pullman) rather than take it simply as fact. That is, we do not source-tag the claim that the sun rises in the East, regardless of who first told us about this, because we quickly learn that we do not need to take the claim under advisement. Whereas when someone tells us a story about an alethiometer, we ask ourselves whether our interlocutor might be making things up, and we attribute the story solely to him or her.

I will return to the question of source-tagging when I take up *Don Quixote*; first, I need to address the more general question of the relation of characters-who-narrate to the narratives they inhabit. It turns out that the problem of the "unreliable narrator"—to which Zunshine devotes a great deal of attention, and which involves our readerly capacities for source-tagging—is actually relatively simple, compared to the question of how to compare Lyra's or Odysseus's capacities for narrative fabulation with those of Benjy or Lennie. Wayne Booth touches lightly on this question in *The Rhetoric of Fiction*, but only to distinguish capable narrators from those "not fully qualified" to take on the job:

> The range of human types that have been dramatized as narrators is almost as great as the range of other fictional characters—one must say "almost" because there are some characters who are not fully qualified to narrate or "reflect" a story (Faulkner can use the idiot for part of his novel only because the other three parts exist to set off and clarify the idiot's jumble). (152)

There is no need now to revisit the question of whether "the idiot's jumble" is merely a jumble, or whether the idiot is just an idiot, or whether Benjy's narrative really requires the prosthesis of the other three parts; we have already established Benjy's capacities as a conscious narrator, however limited they might be. For the purposes of this chapter, it suffices to acknowledge that—as we saw with Michael

K—those who cannot represent themselves must be represented, and that—as we saw in *The Woman Warrior*—intellectually disabled characters can "haunt" all narrative by serving as examples of humans who cannot fully account for themselves.

It is in this sense that such characters are not "fully qualified" to serve as narrators, but I think there is much to be gained by seeing them on a spectrum with skilled fabulists such as Lyra and Odysseus. Not only does this allow readers to apprehend the ways all narratives comment, implicitly or explicitly, on their own operations; it also allows us to better understand what is at stake when characters who are "not fully qualified" to narrate become central to their own narrative. There are two options here: such characters can try to narrate their own stories, or they can be the subjects of stories narrated by others. Under the latter heading, take "poor Stevie" from Conrad's *Secret Agent*. Stevie's fate is horrible: he is blown to bits while on a mission he cannot begin to comprehend, dispatched by his brother-in-law, Verloc, to blow up the Greenwich Observatory in a staged act of terrorism that will (as Verloc's embassy contact and superior, Mr. Vladimir, hopes) be blamed on anarchists and lead to a national-security clampdown in England. Admittedly, Stevie's failure to understand his role in the narrative is not necessarily attributable to his intellectual disability; the plot to blow up the Greenwich Observatory was designed by Mr. Vladimir to be misread by everyone, and only the perspicacity of the Assistant Commissioner manages to pierce the veil of deception and discern that "the London anarchists had nothing to do with this" (90), whereas Chief Inspector Head remains determined to follow the only plot line he can discern, the one that leads (wrongly) to the London anarchist Michaelis. But Stevie's violent death is tragic and pathetic nonetheless, not least because Verloc finds him so easy to dupe (even if he does not intend for Stevie to be killed—the boy trips and falls, setting off the explosion prematurely), and because, after his death, Verloc treats Stevie's life as being of so little value. His wife, Winnie, stunned and outraged beyond words, kills her husband for his insouciance, then attempts to run away with the anarchist Comrade Ossipon, who robs and defrauds her; she commits suicide on the way to France.

Clearly, *The Secret Agent* is a narrative with intellectual disability as its motive, and could have been discussed in these terms in chapter 1; for once Winnie has stabbed her husband to death, the narrative reveals, in an extended reverie, that protecting Stevie has been Winnie's lifelong mission, going back to her childhood and her violently abusive father:

> She remembered brushing the boy's hair and tying his pinafores—herself in a pinafore still; the consolations administered to a small and badly scared creature by another creature nearly as small but not quite so badly scared; she had the vision of the blows intercepted (often with her own head), of a door held desperately shut against a man's rage (not for very long); of a poker flung once (not very far), which stilled that particular storm into the dumb and awful silence which follows a thunder-clap. And all these scenes of violence came and went accompanied by the unrefined noise of deep vociferations proceeding from a man wounded in his paternal pride, declaring himself obviously accursed since one of his kids was a "slobbering idjut and the other a wicked she-devil." (200)

As in *Life and Times of Michael K, The Sound and the Fury,* and *Martian Time-Slip*, the initial plot premise (the Greenwich Observatory, the decline of the Compsons, the need to bring Anna K to her place of birth, the plan for the F.D.R. Mountains) is supplanted, or at least challenged, by talk of genocide, as the anarchist Professor closes the novel with a profoundly delusional eliminationist rant:

"Do you understand, Ossipon? The root of all evil! They are our sinister masters—the weak, the flabby, the silly, the cowardly, the faint of heart, and the slavish of mind. They have the power. They are the multitude. Theirs is the kingdom of the earth. Exterminate, exterminate! That is the only way of progress. It is! Follow me, Ossipon? First the great multitude of the weak must go, then the only relatively strong. You see? First the blind, then the deaf and the dumb, then the halt and the lame—and so on. Every taint, every vice, every prejudice, every convention must meet its doom." (247)

The delusional part of this rant, of course, lies in the Professor's conviction that the weak are the masters, when in fact, at his point in history and for the next few decades, they are the objects of various eugenicist agendas carried out by the real masters of society, one branch of which eventually decided that they constituted a master race. It was surely a bit too heavy-handed of Conrad to underscore the point by making the Professor a "bespectacled, dingy little man" (62), dwarfish in stature, "no taller than the seated Ossipon" (74). The Professor promotes a vision of the world in which, despite his delusions, he will not become an übermensch; he will be fodder. Needless to say, the greater fool he. But the focal point of the plot remains Stevie.

As has been evident throughout this book, my analytical categories are not hermetically sealed; disability-as-motive in *The Woman Warrior* eventually leaks into disability-and-self-awareness, and the formal experiments in Philip K. Dick's *Martian Time-Slip* are not only examples of textual self-awareness and alternate modes of rendering temporality, but also (indirectly, but ultimately) referable to the novel's plot. Any narrative that deploys intellectual disability as a means of exploring narrative time can also use intellectual disability as motive—and may even do so self-reflexively. *The Secret Agent* is all about motive; the reason I have saved the novel for my discussion of self-awareness, however, stems from a single passage that follows Winnie Verloc's memory of protecting Stevie from their father:

> It was a crushing memory, an exhausting vision of countless breakfast trays carried up and down innumerable stairs, of endless haggling over pence, of the endless drudgery of sweeping, dusting, cleaning, from basement to attics; while the impotent mother, staggering on swollen legs, cooked in a grimy kitchen, and poor Stevie, *the unconscious presiding genius of all their toil,* blacked the gentlemen's boots in the scullery. (200; my emphasis)

All we know about Stevie's cognitive capacities is that he has a visceral horror of cruelty (to people or to animals), and that he is capable of perceiving that this is a "bad world for poor people" (146). Left to himself, he draws endless circles on paper; we will see a version of this behavior later on in *Foe*, with Friday's drawings of eerie walking eyes, a similar device by which an enigmatic character with an unspecified intellectual disability offers cryptic, mute commentary on his surroundings. But the idea that Stevie is the "unconscious presiding genius" goes well beyond the immediate invocation of his sister's and mother's ceaseless and underappreciated toil; though the term "genius," as applied to Stevie, is perhaps as heavy-handed as Conrad's rendering of the Professor (despite the term's otherwise benign overtones of Stevie as *genius loci*), it is possible to say that Stevie *is* in fact the unconscious presiding genius of the entire novel, as Lyra and Odysseus are the conscious presiding geniuses of their narratives.

Now we have come to wide and open terrain, the ground I hoped to reach by juxtaposing Stevie to Odysseus and Lyra Belacqua. For the question of what a character knows about the narrative she or he inhabits is by no means limited to characters with intellectual disabilities: it is the foundation of narrative irony, as central to *Oedipus Rex* as to *The Speed of Dark*. In the former, the question of whether Oedipus understands the narrative he inhabits is nothing less than the central question of the play; it is so fundamental to the structure of the plot that it is impossible to imagine anyone—even on the play's opening night, with a nervous Sophocles watching in the wings—thinking, "I hope we find out who killed Laius and brought this plague upon Thebes" (spoiler alert: *it was Oedipus all along!*). But the narrative irony is much harder to pull off when the character with an intellectual disability is one of those "not fully qualified" narrators; with Benjy Compson, the narrative's experiments with temporality take precedence (on my reading) over the question of what he knows about the narrative he is in, though certainly that question cannot and should not be ignored altogether. By contrast, as I mentioned briefly in the introduction, the narrative of Elizabeth Moon's *Speed of Dark* turns almost exclusively on what Lou Arrendale knows and can know. Unfortunately, the question of whether Lou, an adult with autism, understands what is happening at his workplace (and to his life) proves so difficult to handle that Moon has to resort to episodic "breaks" narrated by a traditionally omniscient narrator, focalized through neurotypical characters (Tom and Pete Aldrin) who have none of Lou's limitations. Lou works at a bioinformatics firm that employs people with autism for their pattern recognition abilities; they are known as Section A, and the firm offers extensive facilities (including a gym with trampolines) to accommodate their special needs. Gene Crenshaw is a manager who wants to get rid of all these allegedly expensive accommodations and subject the members of Section A to experimental treatments that will cure their autism. But since Lou doesn't know about any of that, another more expository level of narrative is provided from the perspective of his coworker Pete Aldrin, who does.[1]

The Speed of Dark explicitly opens and closes with the question of who knows what about whom, and who is thereby authorized to ask questions and validate answers. The narrator in the passage below is Lou, and he is registering his (fruitless) objections to the endless barrage of psychiatric evaluations to which he is subjected:

> Questions, always questions. They didn't wait for the answers, either. They rushed on, piling questions on questions, covering every moment with questions, blocking off every sensation but the thorn stab of questions. . . . Dr. Fornum, crisp and professional, raises an eyebrow and shakes her head not quite imperceptibly. Autistic persons do not understand these signals; the book says so. I have read the book, so I know what it is I do not understand.
>
> What I haven't figured out is the range of things they don't understand. The normals. The reals. The ones who have the degrees and sit behind the desks in comfortable chairs. . . . She doesn't want to know what I mean. She wants me to say what other people say. "Good morning, Dr. Fornum." "Yes, I'm fine, thank you." "Yes, I can wait. I don't mind." (1–2)

Lou eventually decides to volunteer for the experimental cure; the epilogue, written seven years afterward, suggests that the treatment has been "successful," even though it has stripped Lou of his feelings for Marjory, a neurotypical woman with whom he had been in love. The last line of the novel, fittingly, is "Now I get to ask the questions" (340); now, too, Lou needs no secondary diegetic device to explain his life.

Whether or not one is happy with Lou's decision—and some readers have objected to it, on the grounds that "cures" for autism should be categorically refused, even in fiction[2]—the point remains that the novel opens with a Lou who does not understand the larger narrative structuring his life, and ends with a Lou who does. For Lou, Benjy, Stevie, and Oedipus, in other words, narrative irony—the distance between what we know as spectators or readers and what they know as characters—constitutes the very fabric of the narrative (as it does for *The Curious Incident of the Dog in the Night-Time*, as well). But this phenomenon is heightened when the character in question has an intellectual disability, not only because of the possibility that other characters might be exploiting that disability to their own advantage (this provides the structure of *Memento*, and the tragedy of *The Secret Agent*) but also because the inability of characters with intellectual disabilities to understand the narratives they inhabit appears, in contrast to Oedipus's hubris, as radical innocence. (Again, think of Steinbeck's Lennie.) We feel pity and terror, as Aristotle suggested, at watching our fellow humans flail about in a world they do not fully understand, subject as they are to their passions, their blood feuds, and their capricious and vengeful gods. But our fellow humans with intellectual disabilities are more vulnerable, more precarious than Oedipus; and if theorists from Aristotle to Freud to Ricoeur to Teresa de Lauretis are right in seeing fundamental narrative principles at stake in the unfolding of Oedipus's story, then perhaps the narrative irony at work in stories involving characters with intellectual disabilities can tell us something important about irony, self-awareness, and self-reflexivity as well as about intellectual disability.[3]

* * *

I trust that I have already made clear, and more than clear, my aversion to diagnosing characters. But I have to reemphasize that aversion here, especially with regard to *Curious Incident* and *The Speed of Dark*, because so much commentary has focused largely on whether the narrators in question are accurate representations of persons with autism; and that commentary, unfortunately, has been explicitly licensed by the novels themselves (and their marketing materials). *Curious Incident* notes, in its front matter, that "Mark Haddon is a writer and illustrator of numerous award-winning children's books and television screenplays. As a young man, Haddon worked with autistic individuals" (n.p.).[4] *The Speed of Dark* makes much of Moon's status as the mother of a young man with autism: the lead blurb on the back cover of the Ballantine paperback (provided courtesy of the *Denver Post*) states that "Moon is the mother of an autistic teenager and her love is apparent in the story of Lou." The novel also features a "reader's guide," an appendix consisting of an interview between Moon and Paul Witcover, that is devoted chiefly to questions about autism, and does not fail to include the perfunctory "I know you have an autistic son; how much of Lou is based on your son and your experiences in raising him?" (n.p.).

But I can anticipate the objection to my diagnosis-aversion when it comes to texts like these: *The Speed of Dark* quite literally announces itself as a novel about autism, and though *Curious Incident* does not, Haddon seems to have outfitted Christopher Boone with every stereotypical marker of someone on the Asperger's end of the autism spectrum—aversion to touch, asocial behaviors, inability to read facial expressions, preternatural facility with math, and trouble with the Sally-Anne test, just for starters. (He does, however, understand why he does not pass the Sally-Anne test.) Moreover, it seems that in some quarters, *Curious Incident* has become the go-to book for young-adult fiction dealing with autism (even though it was not considered a YA book when it was published), just as Daniel Keyes's *Flowers for Algernon* wound up selling over five million copies a generation ago by becoming a widely assigned middle and high school text dealing with the matter of what was then called mental retardation. It would seem that autism is literally written onto the pages before us. So why shy away from literalism?

For many reasons, not least of which is that literalism is so (literally) literalist. As I have noted above, the diagnostic mode leads us to conclude that *character X has Y disability* and can thereby preclude us from asking broader interpretive questions about plot and motive (and with *Curious Incident* and *The Speed of Dark*, the temptation becomes all but inevitable: *all autistic people are like that*). The diagnostic mode then leads us away from the grainy details of specific passages and utterances, distracting us from what we should be asking about narrative as such. Mark Osteen offers a useful corrective to this tendency in his introduction to the edited volume *Autism and Representation*. Oddly, he does so even in the course of plaintively asking for more literal representations of people with autism in novels and film: "Is it too much to expect simple accuracy?" (30) Simple accuracy! When was fictional "accuracy" ever simple? When I hear calls for "simple accuracy," I reach for my Aristotle—and then my copy of Beckett's *Molloy*. And Osteen's demand comes, remarkably, in response to Tom Shakespeare's rather reasonable reminder that "it is dangerous to develop hard and fast rules of representation" (qtd. at 30). Nevertheless, despite invoking a mimetic criterion that would hold creative writers to the most naive forms of literalism, Osteen proceeds to show deftly how Mark Haddon's ironic humor works in the text:

> Christopher's inability to comprehend others' emotions also enables Haddon to filter the bathos from potentially overwrought scenes. For example, when Christopher finally arrives at his estranged mother Judy's apartment following a harrowing train journey to London, he informs her that his father, Ed, had told him she was dead. Christopher—a big fan of TV nature shows—blandly tells us, "And then she made a loud wailing noise like an animal on a nature program

on television." Christopher's neutral narration makes the scene more powerful. (39)

That it does, clearly enough. (I confirmed this, at least to my own satisfaction, by seeing the stage version of *Curious Incident*, in which I found Christopher's parents' moments of anguish less compelling for being directly represented to us by their characters.) Moreover, it is the key to reading the book: Christopher's neutral narration compels us to read over his shoulder, so to speak, particularly with regard to his interactions with the novel's other characters:

> And I asked the policeman, "How much does it cost to get a ticket for a train to London?"
> And he said, "About 30 quid."
> And I said, "Is that pounds?"
> And he said, "Christ alive," and he laughed. But I didn't laugh because I don't like people laughing at me, even if they are policemen. (151)

This structure, whereby readers must supply the missing connective tissue that explains *why* the policeman laughed and said "Christ alive," subtends nearly every one of Christopher's exchanges—with his father, about whether he is crying because he is sad about Wellington ("Yes, Christopher, you could say that. You could very well say that" [21], he replies, rather than explaining that he is sad about the breakup of his marriage and his relationship with Mrs. Shears), with Mrs. Alexander, about why his father does not like Mr. Shears, or with the Indian man in the Underground kiosk about the location of 451c Chapter Road, London NW2 5NG. For diagnostically minded readers, that exchange with the Indian man happens because Christopher has autism; fair enough, but for my purposes the exchange with the Indian man produces a dialogue that reveals just how many implicit nonverbal and social cues can reside in the phrase "two ninety-five," and *that* is the point of the textual operation, regardless of whether Christopher's intellectual disability is represented "accurately":

So I went up to the man in the little shop and I said, "Where is 451c Chapter Road, London NW2 5NG?"

And he picked up a little book and handed it to me and said, "Two ninety five."

And the book was called **London AZ Street Atlas Index, Geographers' A-Z Map Company**, and I opened it up and it was lots of maps.

And the man in the little shop said, "Are you going to buy it or not?"

And I said, "I don't know."

And he said, "Well, you can get your dirty fingers off it if you don't mind," and he took it back from me.

And I said, "Where is 451c Chapter Road, London NW2 5NG?"

And he said, "You can either buy the A-to-Z or you can hop it. I'm not a walking encyclopedia."

And I said, "Is that the A-to-Z?" and I pointed at the book.

And he said, "No, it's a sodding crocodile."

And I said, "Is that the A-to-Z?" because it wasn't a crocodile and I thought I had heard wrong because of his accent.

And he said, "Yes, it's the A-to-Z."

And I said, "Can I buy it?"

And he didn't say anything.

And I said, "Can I buy it?"

And he said, "Two pounds ninety-five, but you're giving me the money first. I'm not having you scarpering," and then I realized that he meant £2.95 when he said *Two ninety-five*. (186–87)

Comic (and/or painful) though it is, this conversation is also a pointed commentary on the limits of literalism—for Christopher's difficulties in understanding the communicative protocols of a simple commercial transaction (on a literal reading of this exchange), but perhaps also for readers inclined to read representations of intellectual disability exclusively as representations of intellectual disability.[5]

Now that we are talking about textual operations rather than about character diagnoses, I want to linger for a moment on the fact that Christopher's "harrowing train journey to London" takes up about one-third of the book. That in itself is remarkable, or should be: where a neurotypical narrator might say, "And then I went by train to my mother's house in London," Christopher recounts the entire journey in minute detail for over sixty pages.[6] The narrative is thrilling, as we learn from Christopher's perspective just how harrowing his journey is; but at the same time, it forces us to reconsider our ordinary distinction between significant and insignificant detail. If I were to tell you about my most recent travels in New York City subways, you would consider it odd if I included in my narrative a detail like the one Christopher provides about the London Underground:

> there were signs saying **Great Western** and **cold beers and lagers** and **CAUTION WET FLOOR** and **Your 50p will keep a premature baby alive for 1.8 seconds** and **transforming travel** and **Refreshingly Different** and **IT'S DELICIOUS IT'S CREAMY AND IT'S ONLY £1.30 HOT CHOC DELUXE** and **0870 777 7676** and **The Lemon Tree** and **No Smoking** and **FINE TEAS**. (145–46)

But in Christopher's narrative, these details make perfect sense, not only because he habitually notices things that neurotypical people miss ("most people are almost blind," he remarks [144], in a nice piece of disability détournement), but also because the constant threat of

sensory overload is part of what makes Christopher's journey so harrowing, as when all the signs turn to gibberish (gubbish?) on the page
"because there were too many and my brain wasn't working properly"
(170). As we have seen time and again, intellectually disabled characters can do that: like Manfred Steiner, they can bend the narrative
around themselves so as to warp our expectations for degrees of detail
or continuity. It is something of a relief, then, when Christopher
finally ends his epic train journey and walks the remaining way to his
mother's house, but cuts back on what most readers would consider
irrelevant detail: "So I started walking, but Siobhan said I didn't have
to describe everything that happens, I just have to describe the things
that were interesting" (189).

The things that *are* interesting as we approach Christopher's desti-
nation, I suspect, include questions like, *What is Christopher's mother's life like with Mr. Shears? How will they manage to accommodate
Christopher in their household?* (Spoiler alert: they don't.) *What will
happen when Christopher's father arrives to try to retrieve him?* But I
have a meta-question about what is and is not "interesting": *How can
it be that we are reading a detective novel written by a teenager who
cannot distinguish significant from insignificant detail?* Doesn't this
violate the very mechanism of detective fiction, articulated by Conan
Doyle's *ars poetica* of detective and novelist, the interpretive operation of separating the essential elements of plot from the irrelevant?
Haddon could not have made matters more explicit: his protagonist
is a Sherlock Holmes fan who deliberately sets out to write a murder
mystery, and who knows that the solution to murder mysteries turns
on the capacity of the detective to function as an information-sorting
demon. At one point Christopher comes upon a detail that he thinks
might be an important clue to who killed Wellington—"either that,"
he writes, "or it was a *Red Herring*, which is a clue which makes you
come to a wrong conclusion or something which looks like a clue

but isn't" (31). What we have in Christopher, then, is a curious set of textual capacities for a detective: on the one hand, a keenly observant eye, a brilliant memory for detail, and an awareness of the distinction between legitimate clues and red herrings; on the other hand, an inability to sort sensory information, an inability to tell when people (such as his father) are lying to him, and an inability to understand motive.

Now we are getting at why—for me, at least, and I hope for you—the self-reflexivity of *Curious Incident* should take interpretive precedence over the question of the "accuracy" of Haddon's representation of a person on the autism spectrum. At the very least, we need (if we are literary critics) to stop ourselves from reading right past the text to the "content" within; though *The Speed of Dark* and *Curious Incident* are both "about" autism and autistic narrators in a baseline sense, these texts differ in substantial and important ways. To begin with, from start to finish, *Curious Incident* is about texts; the title itself, remarking an absence (the absence of sound from the dog who does not bark in the night), announces its relation to the Sherlock Holmes story "Silver Blaze," and Christopher tells us in so many words that "I do like murder mystery novels. So I am writing a murder mystery novel" (5). He pointedly contrasts murder mystery novels with "proper novels," which he does not like—and he briefly explains why: "In proper novels people say things like, 'I am veined with iron, with silver and with streaks of common mud. I cannot contract into the firm fist which those clench who do not depend on stimulus.' What does this mean? I do not know. Nor does Father. Nor does Siobhan or Mr. Jeavons. I have asked them" (4–5).

To be honest, I don't know what this passage means, either. But I do know it comes from *The Waves*, by Virginia Woolf, hardly a proper novel. So what is the point of this sly literary-history joke, and why should *Curious Incident* announce its relation to improperly "proper" novels in its opening pages? It is not just a matter of determining whether *The Waves* constitutes a "proper novel," though we will revisit the question of what we mean by "proper" novels in the course of discussing *Don Quixote, Pale Fire,* and *Foe.* The larger point, obviously, is that the neurotypical characters in *Curious Incident* aren't any better at reading that passage than Christopher is. It is as if, in the face of *The Waves,* no one in *Curious Incident* is any more or less intellectually disabled than anyone else. That possibility in turn opens onto the novel's implicit but profound suggestion that no one in Christopher's world, with the possible exception of Siobhan, his paraprofessional aide, is any less socially maladroit than he is. As James Berger writes, "The social order is itself firmly placed on the autism spectrum," inasmuch as it "is characterized by its members' isolation and inability to communicate with each other" (201). This is an appropriate "thematic" reading of *Curious Incident*'s intertextual relation to *The Waves,* cuing us to the fact that the novel will be full of misunderstandings and misreadings, beginning with Christopher's misreading of the central mystery to which the death of Wellington the dog is epiphenomenal. But it is critical, for my purposes, that the cue is one of relation between text and text.

Christopher, for his part, does not know he is in a fictional text, though he is narratively self-aware; as he writes of his brief stay in a police cell, "I wondered how I would escape if I was in a story" (14). However, he is writing the text as he goes along, and rereading as he goes, such that he can write in chapter 181, "I realize that I told a lie in **Chapter 13** because I said 'I cannot tell jokes,' because I do know 3 jokes that I can tell and I understand and one of them is about a cow, and Siobhan said I don't have to go back and change what I wrote in **Chapter 13** because it doesn't matter because it is not a lie, just a *clarification*" (142–43). So the text has an explicit and ongoing relationship to itself throughout. Indeed, about a third of the way through *Curious*

Incident, there is a curious incident: Christopher's father discovers the book Christopher is writing, and realizes that Christopher is trying to find out who killed Wellington, even though he has expressly and repeatedly forbidden Christopher to do so. When Christopher replies to the effect that he has faithfully followed the letter of his father's instructions if not their spirit, his father replies, "Don't give me that bollocks, you little shit. You knew exactly what you were bloody doing. I've read the book, remember" (81).

Ed Boone has, in other words, read the book we have been reading. There ensues a complex intratextual period during which Ed confiscates the book and hides it, which leads one to ask where, exactly, Christopher is writing down the story of how he looked for the book while his father was out of the house. But that question is quickly superseded by yet another level of textuality in the narrative. When Christopher finds his book hidden in the closet of his father's bedroom, he thinks,

> I decided that I would leave the book where it was because I reasoned that Father wasn't going to throw it away if he had put it into the shirt box and I could carry on writing in another book that I would keep secret [presumably that is where this passage has been recorded] and then, maybe later, he might change his mind and let me have the first book back again and I could copy the new book into it. And if he never gave it back to me I would be able to remember most of what I had written, so I would put it all into the second secret book and if there were bits I wanted to check to make sure I had remembered them correctly I could come into his room when he was out and check. (94)

Just as *Curious Incident*'s relation to its own status as a text is verging on *Quixote*-level involution, Christopher finds the texts that will help him solve two mysteries—the mystery of who killed Wellington, and the mystery of what his narrative is really about. For in finding his mother's letters to him, which his father had kept from him in order to maintain the cover story that his mother is dead, Christopher discovers that he had not, in fact, understood the narrative he inhabits. Here, then, the narrative's self-reflexivity doubles back onto the question of whether the intellectually disabled character can understand his/her own narrative and serve as a "fully qualified" narrator.

Emotionally, for Christopher (and, I suspect, for many readers), the effect is devastating: his father has been lying to him, his mother is alive, his mother abandoned him and ran off with Mr. Shears. *That* is the real story; that is the reason Ed Boone told his son that his mother had "a problem with her heart" (23)—a passage we learn to reread only when we have read Judy Boone's letters. But as a formal, compositional matter, Judy's letters represent an ingenious solution to the problem Elizabeth Moon grappled with in *The Speed of Dark*, the problem of how an intellectually disabled character can come to understand the broader parameters of the story s/he is telling. Moon's solution was to invent more narrators; Haddon's is to invent more texts.

* * *

At this point we can ask why textual self-awareness and self-reflexivity should be of especial interest in a narrative whose protagonist has a cognitively atypical relation to narrative—and I can return to Lisa Zunshine's work on metarepresentation. One of the questions that arises when we have a detective who cannot tell when people are lying to him is this: What happens if we posit a person with a cognitive disability that prevents him or her from source-tagging? What if we imagined a reader—or, more interestingly, a character who is not a narrator—with no capacity for metarepresentation, who cannot distinguish fiction from fact? We might get the Thermians from the film *Galaxy Quest*, who call upon the cast of a long-since-cancelled TV science-fiction show to save them from genocide because they believe the show's episodes to be, in their terms, the "historical documents." Or we might get Don Quixote.

And if we get Don Quixote, then we get the novel *Don Quixote*—and that has some interesting implications not only for our metarepresentational capacities (or lack thereof) but also for the way a disabled metarepresentational capacity can produce metafiction. Zunshine cites the neuropsychiatrist Christopher Frith to the effect that "self-awareness cannot occur without metarepresentation," that is, the "cognitive mechanism that enables us to be aware of our goals, our intentions, and the intentions of other people" (qtd. at 55). But Zunshine does not pursue what this might mean for textual representations of characters who lack the capacity for metarepresentation, even though she mentions Don Quixote briefly. Cervantes's representation of Don Quixote, after all, is not simply the spectacle of a man so addled by his reading of chivalric romances that he is willing to tilt at windmills, though this is by far the most common image of the character. Rather, what makes *Don Quixote* interesting in this respect is Cervantes' gambit of making Book 2 an extended metacommentary on Book 1, by introducing Don Quixote and Sancho Panza to a world in which untold thousands of people all across Europe have read a book titled *The Ingenious Gentleman Don Quixote of La Mancha*.

Cervantes's readers will recall the "ridiculous conversation"—for so it is titled in the headnote to chapter 3 of Book 2—that takes place between Don Quixote, Sancho Panza, and Sansón Carrasco, after Sancho meets Carrasco and learns that Carrasco has somehow read all about him. Just before Carrasco's arrival, Don Quixote wonders how such a book can have been produced, since it is less than a month since he returned home at the close of Book 1, and he worries to himself about how he has been portrayed in this book. He consoles himself with the thought that "if, however, it were true that such history was in existence, seeing that it was about a knight-errant, it must of necessity be grandiloquent, lofty, distinguished, and true" (544). Let us attend first to the recursivity here: if it is true that such a book exists, then, given its subject matter, the narrative must be true. We are already in a hall of mirrors, because Book 1 started out with Don Quixote narrating to himself the manner in which his adventures will be narrated, and after the narrative trails off in mid-episode in chapter 8, Cervantes continues the novel by "discovering" the manuscript, "History of Don Quixote of La Mancha, written by a Cide Hamete Benengali, Arabian historian." (Perhaps this is the secret second book, analogous to Christopher Boone's.) So within the fictional universe of Book 2 of *Don Quixote*, it is in fact true that there is a book about Don Quixote (which we know as Book 1), and that book even contains evidence of *another* true book about Don Quixote, written by an Arab historian, though at one point Cervantes very wisely cautions us to take such claims with a grain of salt, because Arabs "are much inclined to lying" (109). And of course within that fictional frame of reference, everything in the first book of *Don Quixote* is "true," just as it is "true" that Lyra Belacqua is good at reading the alethiometer and at telling lies to talking armored bears. It cannot be otherwise: the book we hear about in Book 2 is in fact the book we have just read, we know it exists, and when Carrasco arrives, he, Sancho, and Don Quixote proceed to discuss the properties of this book as well as its popular and critical reception.

When Carrasco mentions that some readers have objected to the inclusion of a small inset novel in Book 1, "The Tale of Ill-Advised Curiosity," taking up chapters 33–35, Don Quixote objects strenuously: "Now I am sure . . . that the author of my story is no sage but some ignorant prater who set himself blindly and aimlessly to write it down and let it turn out anyhow" (549). Apparently, the narrator of *Don Quixote* has no capacity for distinguishing significant from insignificant detail, and is incapable of writing a proper novel; Martin Amis has emphatically agreed, writing that "reading *Don Quixote* can be compared to an indefinite visit from your most impossible senior relative, with all his pranks, dirty habits, unstoppable reminiscences, and terrible cronies" (427). But nestled safely within the garrulous text of *Don Quixote*, Carrasco assures Quixote that there is no cause for concern, for "this story, in fact, is the most delightful and least harmful entertainment ever seen to this day," whereupon Quixote replies, "To write in any other way . . . would be to write not truths but lies, and historians who resort to lying ought to be burned like coiners of false money. But I do not know what induced the author to make use of novels and irrelevant tales when he had so much to write of in mine" (549). The remainder of Book 2 is based on the premise that the characters in Book 2 have read Book 1, and are willing to humor Don Quixote accordingly; and matters take a still stranger turn when, in 1614, Cervantes gets word of Alonso Fernández de Avellaneda's spurious Book 2 (a counterfeit lie, told by a counterfeit coiner of false money), and decides to work that text into his own. In chapter 59, headed "In which is recorded the extraordinary event that might pass for an adventure of Don Quixote," Sancho and Quixote stop at an inn in which they hear someone say, "I beseech you, till supper is brought in, let us read another chapter of the second part of *Don Quixote of La Mancha*" (949). Our heroes burst in on their fellow-travelers; Quixote flips through the book and pronounces it "wholly stupid" (952), and his interlocutors note that the scene of Don Quixote's appearance at the tournament in Saragossa is "a measly account, defective in contrivance, mean in style, wretchedly poor in devices, and rich only in absurdities" (953).

The infinite self-reflexivity of *Don Quixote* is made possible chiefly by the fact that the two books were published ten years apart, but it makes sense, when one's protagonist is unable to distinguish fiction from nonfiction, that the fiction he inhabits should explore the parameters and presuppositions of fiction. This aspect of *Don Quixote* has been commented on from the moment the real (that is, not the fictional) Book 2 of *Don Quixote* appeared, and the idea that *Don Quixote* is a novel about the writing of *Don Quixote* has resonated for centuries, all the way to Borges's "Pierre Menard, Author of the *Quixote*," in which "Menard's fragmentary *Quixote*"—which is no less than an exact word-for-word recreation of the original—is judged to be "more subtle than Cervantes'" (42). But it is striking that no one has framed this question in terms of disability: Don Quixote is intellectually disabled. He has become synonymous with a kind of madness, the madness of one who takes fiction for reality. And yet his disability, which is inevitably a *textual* disability, winds up producing a text, Book 2, in which his delusions effectively become real. This is also the premise of Pirandello's *Henry IV*, although there, the Italian actor whose family is going to great lengths to honor his apparent delusion that he is Henry IV, Holy Roman Emperor (a delusion that began on the day he played Henry IV in a pageant), has in fact recovered from that delusion years before the action of the play begins, and has now chosen to live *as if* he is suffering from the delusion that he is Henry IV. But Don Quixote's delusion is based on his relation to texts, so that the premise of Book 1 of *Don Quixote*—that a dotty old country gentleman gets it into his head that the chivalric romances written three centuries earlier are in fact historical accounts of a world that needs to be revived today—turns, in Book 2, into a world where everyone behaves as if the chivalric romances written three centuries earlier are in fact historical accounts of a world that needs to be revived today. The disability, Don Quixote's lack of a metarepresentational capacity, warps the text, turning it back on itself in a dizzying series of metafictional reflections on the nature of fiction and the nature of reflection—just as Christopher's father has read the book you have read up to the point at which Christopher narrates to us his father's discovery of the book, and just as *Henry IV* and Henry IV reflect on "reflection," mental and physical ("When I was a child, I thought the moon in the pond was real" [193]).

Something similar, though on a much smaller scale, happens in *Galaxy Quest*. *Galaxy Quest* also opens in a metafictional mode, with an old episode of the show being screened at a *Galaxy Quest* convention; it is from the start a film about *Star Trek* and *Star Trek* fandom. It is also deeply literate about the clichés of popular science fiction—the reptilian aliens, the mysterious Omega-13 substance, the escape through the ducts of the ship ("Why is it always ducts?" asks Sigourney Weaver, nodding at one of the tropes of the film *Aliens*), the unnamed crewmember who dies before the first commercial break, the self-destruct mechanism aborted at the last instant, and the obligatory magical unobtainium substance that makes interstellar travel possible (the beryllium sphere).[7] But once the narrative centers on characters—the Thermians—who lack the metarepresentational capacity to distinguish fact from fiction, a funny thing happens. The film's labyrinths are not as rich or elaborate as those of the *Quixote*, but they do induce a hyperawareness of the fictional nature of the fiction we are watching (even though the idea that the events within that fiction are "real" to the characters is, as in *Curious Incident*, never abandoned), inasmuch as the film's denouement turns on all the plot clichés the film has been satirizing. Where Quixote's misreading of chivalric fiction as history parodically reanimates the clichés of late medieval romances, the Thermians' belief in the veracity of the historical documents redeems all the clichés of mainstream science fiction, as the narrative stages its relation to its own genre by revivifying all the dead elements with which it began. The coup de grace in *Galaxy Quest*, for the fan narrative, comes when the teenage fan who approached the captain at the *Galaxy Quest* convention with an arcane question about the ship, and who was angrily rebuffed by the actor playing the captain ("There's no quantum flux, there's no auxiliary, *there's no goddamn ship*"), saves the crew from destruction thanks to the minutely detailed blueprints of the ship he and his friends have stored on their hard drives.

Each of these narratives—*Curious Incident, Don Quixote, Henry IV*, and *Galaxy Quest*—involves a character or characters (in one case, a narrator) whose intellectual disability entails a diminished or nonexistent capacity for metarepresentation, and who thereby (a) produce metafictional textual effects, and (b) in the course of producing metafictional effects, break their narratives' fictional frame in such a way as to confirm it. Christopher, believing he is writing a murder mystery novel about a dog, uncovers in the course of his "detections" a real mystery, whereby his narrative becomes an adventure story of an epic journey to London. Quixote, living among the characters in Book 2 who have read the first book you have just read, creates a narrative in which his delusions reshape the world. The Thermians, believing in the reality of the *N.S.E.A. Protector*, create an actual version of it that allows the fictional world of "Galaxy Quest" to become a real world within the fictional world of *Galaxy Quest*; *Henry IV* offers a variation on the theme, in which the mad king decides, upon regaining his senses, that he would rather remain—for his own amusement and edification, and for revenge against his family—in the fictional world they have created for him. In each case, intellectual disability becomes the occasion or the device for forging a link between the mechanics of metarepresentation and the machinations of metafiction.

It is therefore possible to see why Nabokov's *Pale Fire* would be germane to this discussion, even though Charles Kinbote, like Don

Quixote, is not usually considered to be a person with an intellectual disability. Like *Henry IV*, though to a considerably greater degree, the text is explicitly about reflection and resemblance; much is made of the pun on Zembla and Zemblans, and the title itself alludes to a passage in *Timon of Athens* on the subject of reflection: "the moon's an arrant thief, / And her pale fire she snatches from the sun" (IV.iii. 437–38). In this light, Kinbote's protestation that "I have no desire to twist and batter an unambiguous *apparatus criticus* into the monstrous semblance of a novel" (86) is this novel's wry (or merely cute?) statement of its own *ars poetica*. A more sustained metacritical moment appears in Kinbote's aside on the work of the painter Eystein:

> While unable to catch a likeness, and therefore wisely limiting himself to a conventional style of complimentary portraiture, Eystein showed himself to be a prodigious master of the trompe l'oeil in the depiction of various objects surrounding his dignified dead models and making them look even deader by contrast to the fallen petal or the polished panel that he rendered with such love and skill. But in some of these portraits Eystein had also resorted to a weird sort of trickery: among his decorations of wood or wool, gold or velvet, he would insert one which was really made of the material elsewhere imitated by paint. (130)

This sounds roughly analogous to what Kinbote's creator, himself a master of trompes l'oeil and weird sorts of textual trickery, is on about in *Pale Fire*; the text is so extravagantly a hall of mirrors that when "a really fantastic mirror" appears in it, a "secret device of reflection," "signed with a diamond by its maker, Sudarg of Bokay" (111), we know at once to hold a mirror up to the mirror and discern there the name of Jakob Gradus, a/k/a Jack Grey, also listed in the index as "Jack Degree, de Grey, d'Argus, Vinogradus, Leningradus, etc." (307).

Ironically yet fittingly, therefore, Kinbote repudiates Eystein's aesthetics as firmly as he repudiates any desire to write a novel:

> This device which was apparently meant to enhance the effect of his tactile and tonal values had, however, something ignoble about it and disclosed not only an essential flaw in Eystein's talent, but the basic fact that "reality" is neither the subject nor the object of true art which creates its own special reality having nothing to do with the average "reality" perceived by the communal eye. (130)

In a weird sort of trickery, Kinbote's criticism of Eystein's aesthetics *also* sounds like an affirmation of Nabokov's own aesthetic; but then, it is difficult to know whether to read Kinbote ironically in this passage, chiefly for the reason that it is difficult to know whether in fact—in the world of the novel—Kinbote actually "exists."

This is the puzzle posed by the notorious final paragraph of this monstrous semblance of a novel, and without the presence of this puzzle, which frames the entire text and raises the question of Kinbote's sanity, the earlier metafictional and metacritical moments of *Pale Fire* would be, I submit, garden-variety twentieth-century experimentalism with no implications for the study of disability in literature. But this adieu compels us to think about whether intellectual disability does, in fact, have a nontrivial relation to the metafictional hijinks for which *Pale Fire* is justly renowned—or infamous:

> God will help me, I trust, to rid myself of any desire to follow the example of two other characters in this work. I shall continue to exist. I may assume other disguises, other forms, but I shall try to exist. I may turn up yet, on another campus, as an old, happy, healthy, heterosexual Russian, a writer in exile, sans fame, sans fortune, sans audience, sans anything but his art. I may join forces with Odon [not to be

confused with Nodo, of course] in a new motion picture: *Escape from Zembla* (ball in the palace, bomb in the palace square). I may pander to the simple tastes of theatrical critics and cook up a stage play, an old-fashioned melodrama with three principals: a lunatic who intends to kill an imaginary king, another lunatic who imagines himself to be that king, and a distinguished old poet who stumbles by chance into the line of fire, and perishes in the clash between the two figments. Oh, I may do many things! History permitting, I may sail back to my recovered kingdom, and with a great sob greet the gray coastline and the gleam of a roof in the rain. I may huddle and groan in a madhouse. (300–301)

The first of these possibilities seems to suggest that Kinbote will turn up as Vladimir Nabokov, teaching in exile at Cornell; the "old-fashioned melodrama" seems to describe reasonably well the drama we have just read, and is usually taken as Nabokov's wink to us. Kinbote, representing himself as King Charles of Zembla, is out of his mind, and Jakob Gradus really is only "Jack Grey, escapee from an asylum, who mistook Shade for the man who sent him there" (299)—not King Charles, of course, but Judge Goldsworth, whose house Kinbote has been renting. But many more possibilities abound, and critics have not failed to explore them. Perhaps Kinbote is really Botkin, a colleague in another department at Wordsmith College; perhaps Kinbote has invented Shade out of whole cloth, and no old poet perishes in the final pages of the poem; perhaps, conversely, Shade has invented Kinbote. It may even be possible that Nabokov has made the whole thing up—that even from the opening page, from the sentence *"Pale Fire*, a poem in heroic couplets, of nine hundred ninety-nine lines, divided into four cantos, was composed by John Francis Shade (born July 5, 1898, died July 21, 1959) during the last twenty days of his life, at his residence in New Wye, Appalachia,

U.S.A." to the sentence "There is a very loud amusement park right in front of my present lodgings," he has been lying to us.[8]

In one sense Kinbote is (if he "exists") a master fabulist, and if he can be described in terms of intellectual disability, he is far more like Quixote than like Christopher Boone. And yet he is almost as clueless in his social exchanges as is Christopher—and to greater comic effect. Whereas Christopher simply does not understand the nonverbal social cues that go into the buying of a street map, Kinbote fails to see that he quickly becomes an object of derision and ridicule. "My free and simple demeanor set everybody at ease," Kinbote writes (21); a bit further on, "Another tormentor inquired if it was true that I had installed two ping-pong tables in my basement. I asked, was it a crime? No, he said, but why two? 'Is *that* a crime?' I countered, and they all laughed" (21–22). Perhaps, then, we are asked to suspect that something is amiss from the very outset, quite apart from the fact that there is a very loud amusement park right in front of Kinbote's present lodgings.

Peter Rabinowitz tried gamely to make sense of this vertigo-inducing text in a 1977 *Critical Inquiry* essay, "Truth in Fiction: A Reexamination of Audiences," in which he set out four levels of readerly immersion in/interpellation by a fictional text. The "actual audience" consists of flesh-and-blood readers holding the book in their hands; the "authorial audience" consists of readers who share the author's historical and cultural assumptions and background; the "narrative audience"—the most important for our purposes, and for Rabinowitz's—consists of members of the actual audience who agree to suspend their disbelief and enter into a work of fiction as if a young girl could talk to armored bears and move across multiple universes with the help of a knife that cuts through the fabric of spacetime; and the "ideal narrative audience" consists of hypothetical people who believe everything a narrator tells them, such that (in Rabinowitz's apt example) the ideal narrative audience of *The Sound and the Fury* "believes that Jason has been victimized and sympathizes with his whining misery, although the narrative audience despises him" (134). The problem with *Pale Fire*, then, is that we simply cannot determine what we need to believe in order to join the narrative audience. The actual and authorial audiences know that Nabokov is making it all up; the ideal narrative audience believes that Charles Kinbote is indeed the exiled king of Zembla and that he became John Shade's dear friend and confidante in the final year of Shade's life. But the narrative audience does not know which of the various interpretive options (Shade and Kinbote both exist, Kinbote is Botkin, Kinbote invented Shade, Shade invented Kinbote) is most plausible:

> Thus, we may say vaguely that *Pale Fire* has something to do with the nature of imagination, the nature of criticism, and the relation of truth to illusion. Yet until we know whether or not Shade and Zembla exist, we cannot know, with any more specificity, just what the novel is doing with these subjects—what questions it is asking, what solutions it is proposing. If both Zembla and Shade exist, we have one novel, probing one set of problems; if Zembla does not exist, but Shade does, we have an entirely different novel, with another set of problems; if . . .
>
> How then is one to read the book? The only way, I suppose, is to make an arbitrary choice about which narrative audience one wants to join—or to read the novel several times, making a different choice each time. As in a game, we are free to make several opening moves; what follows will be dependent upon our initial decision. Simply with respect to the questions suggested above, we can generate four novels, all different but all couched, oddly, in the same words. And as we begin to ask further questions—Has Shade invented Kinbote? Is the poem a good one in the eyes of the narrative audience?—the number of possible novels begins to proliferate at a geometric rate. (140)

Despite the likelihood that Nabokov would shudder at the thought that anyone would ask one of his novels to propose "solutions" to anything, this is a reasonably accurate rendering of the interpretive dilemma posed by Kinbote's instability. One might go so far as to say that just as *Memento* attempts to disable its viewers' sense of causality, *Pale Fire* attempts to disable readers in such a way that they cannot join any one narrative audience with any certainty.

The only question I have is this: why is this a problem? At the very least, by Rabinowitz's reckoning, Nabokov has given us four novels for the price of one. Philip K. Dick did no less, offering us the possibility that *Martian Time-Slip* closes in Arnie Kott's hallucination (a hallucination in which he dies twice), in Jack Bohlen's schizophrenia, in Manfred Steiner's disability chronotope, or in the timespace of the Bleekmen whose entrance into the novel, and whose water witch, warped the text the moment it appeared in the second chapter. For Rabinowitz, the impossibility of joining any one narrative audience presents "an obstacle which prevents us from even the most superficial understanding of the text" (139). But surely this is an unwarranted conclusion, not only because the proliferation of possible texts both invites and follows from (in the reciprocal reader-text loop) the proliferation of possible readings, some of which will go well beyond "even the most superficial understanding," but also because, as I will show at the conclusion of this chapter, there is a potential reading of *Pale Fire* that obtains for all possible scenarios, one that goes to the heart of why any writer would explore the infinite terrain of metafiction by way of the deployment of intellectual disability.

＊ ＊ ＊

To conclude this chapter—and to bring these reflections on textual self-awareness to a (provisional) close—I will turn to a work of metafiction whose (putatively) intellectually disabled character seems to have no control over the production of the text, and whose capacity for metarepresentation is irrelevant to the interpretation of the text. If you like, you might think of this final scenario as an example of what happens when a writer puts Stevie from *The Secret Agent* into a Cervantes-Pirandello-Nabokov-Haddon hall of mirrors: both of this chapter's central questions (What does the character know about the narrative s/he inhabits? Why is the text self-reflexive with regard to intellectual disability?) are animated in such a way as to feed off each other in ways that heighten the hermeneutical impasse of metafiction by means of the hermeneutical impasse of disability. And just for good measure, there will be textual glitches, as well.

I do not need to establish that J. M. Coetzee's *Foe* is a text about texts. Like *Curious Incident* and *Pale Fire*, the title announces its intertextual relations, and as many readers have noted, the explicit rewriting of *Robinson Crusoe* is cross-cut with a less explicit incorporation of the more obscure Defoe novel *Roxana*.[9] Nor do I need to belabor the point that *Foe* is largely a novel about authorship, about who gains control—in what circumstances and with what consequences—over a narrative, one's own or someone else's. The novel devotes many pages to Foe's and Susan Barton's debate over how *Foe* should be written, and on what grounds: "The story I desire to be known by," Susan insists, "is the story of the island." In demanding that Foe leave her life in Bahia out of his account, she says,

> You call it an episode, but I call it a story in its right. It commences with my being cast away there and concludes with the death of Cruso and the return of Friday and myself to England, full of new hope. Within this larger story are inset the stories of how I came to be marooned (told by myself to Cruso) and of Cruso's shipwreck and early years on the island (told by Cruso to myself), as well as the story of Friday, which is properly not a story but a puzzle or hole in the nar-

rative (I picture it as a buttonhole, carefully cross-stitched around, but empty, waiting for the button). Taken in all, it is a narrative with a beginning and an end, and with pleasing digressions too, lacking only a substantial and varied middle, in the place where Cruso spent too much time tilling the terraces and I too much time tramping the shores. Once you proposed to supply a middle by inventing cannibals and pirates. These I would not accept because they were not the truth. Now you propose to reduce the island to an episode in the history of a woman in search of a lost daughter. This too I reject. (121)

Susan Barton opens this prospectus by demanding that the story begin where *Foe* actually does begin, when she is a castaway washed up on the island inhabited by Cruso and Friday. She then proceeds to offer commentary on novels Daniel Defoe has (in the timeframe of *Foe*) not yet written, *Roxana* (with an abandoned daughter named Susan), and of course *Robinson Crusoe* (the version we now know, featuring those fictional cannibals and pirates). Friday's story, like that of Michael K, is not properly a story at all: where Michael K always found a gap, a hole, a darkness when he tried to account for himself, Friday is not even capable of attempting narrative self-representation, and is therefore assigned the role of puzzle or hole by a character who never appears in *Robinson Crusoe* (where, notably, Friday can speak). "Friday has no command of words," Susan tells Foe, "and therefore no defence against being re-shaped day by day in conformity with the desires of others" (121).

Benita Parry has remarked on the phenomenon by which Coetzee grants some narrative agency to Susan Barton while stripping the subaltern subject of his very tongue; "The effects of bestowing authority on the woman's text," she writes, "while withholding discursive skills from the dispossessed, is to reinscribe, indeed re-enact, the received disposal of narrative power, where voice is correlated with cultural supremacy and voicelessness with subjugation" (158). It is as if Coetzee has restored a woman's voice to an eighteenth-century text while leaving the black character with even less autonomy and voice than he had had centuries ago: as Radhika Jones remarks, the novel "accords Friday even less agency than he possessed in the colonial age" (59). (Susan thinks at one point that Foe will decide that Cruso's story is "better without the woman" [72], and we surmise thereby that Defoe did indeed come to that conclusion, and that *Foe* gives us the real story of which *Robinson Crusoe* is but the redaction.) But again, we need to ask specifically about the status of disability in the text. The disability studies reading should supplement, rather than attempt to supplant, the necessary postcolonial reading: for it is not a question of whether the subaltern can speak. This one cannot. The question is what function or functions the nonverbal subaltern, presumed by his fellow characters to be incompetent, to be intellectually disabled, performs in the text. Clearly, Friday is physically disabled, unable to speak ever since someone (slave traders? cannibals? Cruso?) cut out his tongue. The question that consumes Susan Barton is whether Friday is therefore intellectually disabled as well: as she asks Cruso, "Is Friday an imbecile incapable of speech?" (22). Susan reports to Foe that she "found Friday in all matters a dull fellow" (22), but as with the narrator and the mute girl in *The Woman Warrior*, she is not content to leave it at that. He becomes an object of morbid fascination: "I began to look on him—I could not help myself—with the horror we reserve for the mutilated. . . . [I]t was the very secretness of his loss that caused me to shrink from him" (24). Susan spends the remainder of the novel obsessing over the fate of Friday's tongue and Friday's relation to speech: "What I fear most is that after years of speechlessness the very notion of speech may be lost to him" (57). To Foe, she writes, "To tell my story and be silent on Friday's tongue is no better than offering a book for sale with pages in it quietly left empty. Yet the only tongue that can tell Friday's secret is the tongue he has lost!" (67).

Friday is the example *par excellence* of Quayson's category of disability as hermeneutical impasse: his disability is indeed the puzzle, the hole, the vortex around which the entire text of *Foe* swirls until it meets its end in shipwreck. Friday deranges the protocols of representation at every level of the text, even unto the scene in which Susan tries to draw the truth from him by drawing the scene of his mutilation (in two versions, one at the hand of a Moor and one at the hand of Cruso) but gives up in despair at the realization that every aspect of her sketches becomes indeterminate once she shows them to Friday. Of the Cruso sketch, she writes, "I recognized with chagrin that it might also be taken to show Cruso as a beneficent father putting a lump of fish into the mouth of child Friday" (68–69). The Moor sketch is still more ambiguous:

> If there was indeed a slave-trader, a Moorish slave-trader with a hooked knife, was my picture of him at all like the Moor Friday remembered? Are Moors tall and clad in white burnouses? Perhaps the Moor gave orders to a trusty slave to cut out the tongues of the captives, a wizened black slave in a loin-cloth. "Is this a faithful representation of the man who cut out your tongue?"—was that what Friday, in his way, understood me to be asking? If so, what answer could he give but No? And even if it was a Moor who cut out his tongue, his Moor was likely an inch taller than mine, or an inch shorter; wore black or blue, not white; was bearded, not clean-shaven; had a straight knife, not a curved one; and so forth. (70)

So much for the naive belief in "accurate" representation.

Foe is therefore right to suggest that Friday is "the eye of the story" (141), and it is no surprise that when Foe urges Susan to teach Friday to write, on the (illusory) ground that writing evades all disability ("Friday has no speech, but he has fingers. . . . Even if he had no fingers, even if the slavers had lopped them all off, he can hold a stick of charcoal between his toes, or between his teeth, like the beggars on the Strand" [143]), Friday responds by drawing "eyes, open eyes, each set upon a human foot: row upon row upon row of eyes upon feet: walking eyes" (147). If Stevie's endless circles suggested (mutely) the nihilism at the heart of the plot of *The Secret Agent*, Friday's walking eyes suggest that he is (mutely) conscious of his status as Central Textual Enigma.

The text of *Foe* does indeed end in shipwreck, and even—or especially—in this respect, Friday's disability is central to the text's operations. As is evident on almost every page, those operations include metafictional attention to the text's operations, as when Foe suggests to Susan in Quixotian terms that they might be characters in a narrative: "Let us confront our worst fear, which is that we have all of us been called into the world from a different order (which we have now forgotten) by a conjurer unknown to us, as you say I have conjured up your daughter and her companion (I have not)" (135). (The closing parenthetical is hardly reassuring, since Defoe, if not Foe, did conjure up Roxana and her daughter.) Susan does, apparently, win the right to have the story begin where she insists it should, with her arrival on the island, but along the way, Foe offers another theory of fiction, which *Foe* does not entirely repudiate:

"We therefore have five parts in all: the loss of the daughter; the quest for the daughter in Brazil; abandonment of the quest, and the adventure of the island; assumption of the quest by the daughter; and reunion of the daughter with her mother. It is thus that we make up a book: loss, then quest, then recovery; beginning, then middle, then end. As to novelty, this is lent by the island episode—which is properly the second part of the middle—and by the reversal in which the daughter takes up the quest abandoned by her mother. . . .

"The island is not a story in itself," said Foe gently, laying a hand on my knee. "We can bring it to life only by setting it within a larger story. By itself it is no better than a waterlogged boat drifting day after day in an empty ocean till one day, humbly and without commotion, it sinks." (117)

The boat does sink, just after Susan and Foe sink into sleep at the end of part 3. "Who will dive into the wreck?" Susan asks on that final night, referring to the shipwreck that marooned Cruso and Friday but also to the shipwreck that will constitute the conclusion of *Foe* in part 4. "On the island I told Cruso it should be Friday, with a rope about his middle for safety. But if Friday cannot tell us what he sees, is Friday in my story any more than a figuring (or pre-figuring) of another diver?" (142).

Yes, Friday cannot tell us what he sees. That much we know. But, like Manfred Steiner, he can draw—and perhaps, like Manfred, he can produce odd textual effects in the narrative that swirls all around him. *Foe* is festooned with *Martian Time-Slip*-esque repetitions, hiccups, and glitches, beginning with its opening sentences, which present themselves in quotes, as reported speech:

"At last I could row no further. My hands were blistered, my back was burned, my body ached. With a sigh, making barely a splash, I slipped overboard" (5).

Presumably these words are addressed to Foe, though this does not become clear until the final page of section 1, on which Foe is finally addressed directly (45). And then a few pages later, we read this, in doubled quotations, as reported speech of reported speech:

"'Then at last I could row no further. My hands were raw, my back was burned, my body ached. With a sigh, making barely a splash, I slipped overboard and began to swim towards your island.'" (11)

In the enigmatic fourth and final section of the novel, an unnamed narrator twice enters a house (the second time, it bears a plaque reading *Daniel Defoe, Author*) in which lie the bodies of "a woman or a girl" on the landing and Foe and Susan in bed; "Friday, in his alcove, has turned to the wall" (155). The narrator finds a manuscript in a box: "Bringing the candle nearer, I read the first words of the tall, looping script: 'Dear Mr Foe, At last I could row no further'" (155). The text within the text then pulls the narrator under:

> With a sigh, making barely a splash, I slip overboard. Gripped by the current, the boat bobs away, drawn south toward the realm of the whales and eternal ice. Around me on the waters are the petals cast by Friday.
>
> I strike out toward the dark cliffs of the island; but something dull and heavy gropes at my leg, something caresses my arm. I am in the great bed of seaweed: the fronds rise and fall with the swell.
>
> With a sigh, with barely a splash, I duck my head under the water. (155–56)

At this point one almost expects Arnie Kott to put on some Mozart— though perhaps Susan, Foe, and Friday would hear only a hideous racket of screeches and shrieks, like the convulsions of corpses.

This is not the only series of glitches in *Foe*; part 3 opens with Susan Barton making her way into Foe's quarters, noting that "the staircase was dark and mean" (113), and part 4 opens with the enigmatic narrator making his/her way into a house, noting that "the staircase is dark and mean" (153). In the first house-entering of part

4, the narrator writes, "On the landing I stumble over a body . . . a woman or a girl . . . she weighs no more than a sack of straw" (153); in the second s/he writes, "On the landing I stumble over the body, light as straw, of a woman or a girl" (155). In the first section, Susan and Foe are desiccated corpses, their skin "dry as paper" (153); in the second, they "lie face to face, her head in the crook of his arm" (155) . . . until the narrator (with a sigh, with barely a splash) finds a shipwreck in which lie "Susan Barton and her dead captain, fat as pigs in their white nightclothes, their limbs extending stiffly from their trunks, their hands, puckered from long immersion, held out in blessing" (157). Both sections end, appropriately, with the opening of Friday's mouth; the second version announces that "this is not a place of words. Each syllable, as it comes out, is caught and filled with water and diffused. This is a place where bodies are their own signs. It is the home of Friday" (157).

I submit that J. M. Coetzee could not have done much more to glitch his text, to repeatedly glitch the text of *Foe*, to signify on his text's metafictionality by way of repetitions and glitches, or to say nearly the same thing a number of times. More important, this strategy provides an ending (or endings) in which a Nabokovian number of possible novels begins to proliferate at a geometric rate, all of which ultimately establish Friday as the unconscious presiding genius of all the other characters' toils—as well as the toils of the conjurer who has called all of these beings into the world. Only one question remains, for *Foe* and for this chapter. Why? Why should there be an intimate, if sometimes elusive, relation between metafictional self-reflexivity and the fictional depiction and deployment of intellectual disability?

Needless to say, the relationship is not a necessary one: many of the narratives in the world of literature, from *Harry Potter* to *Of Mice and Men* to *The Secret Agent*, manage to make thematic or formal use of intellectual disability without entangling themselves in bewildering disability chronotopes or metafictional Möbius strips. And yet when such narratives *do* entangle themselves in bewildering disability chronotopes, they open onto stunning spatiotemporal vistas that exceed ordinary human comprehension (and can be accessed only by extraordinary human comprehension); when they entangle themselves in metafictional Möbius strips, they open onto profound examinations of the very nature and purpose of self-consciousness.

At this point a literal-minded reader, undeterred by my warnings about literalism, might object that in this chapter the most heterogeneous conditions are yoked by sheer argument together: the autism of Christopher Boone is not the madness of Don Quixote or the feigned madness of Henry IV or the putative madness of Charles Kinbote, and none of the above are equivalent to Friday's condition, which consists of nothing more than the presumption of intellectual disability. To this charge I happily plead guilty, because (once more with feeling) I am not diagnosing these characters, and therefore not claiming that they exhibit similar symptoms under a general heading of Disabled Self-Reflexivity Syndrome. I am claiming instead that their narratives operate in similar ways, and that their *fictional disabilities* are the key to those operations. I could say the same about Manfred Steiner, but I think his textual operations are so closely tied to an intellectual disability chronotope, rather than to textual self-awareness, that I decided that *Martian Time-Slip* would work better in juxtaposition with *The Sound and the Fury*. But the same principle holds for those novels, as well: I am not speculating about the attributes of literary characters. I am calling attention to the operations of literary texts.

And when the operations of literary texts involve implicit and explicit commentary or meditations on the operations of literary texts, I am tempted to conclude—and therefore I will—that there seems to be a nontrivial relation between the kind of self-consciousness necessary for metarepresentation and the kind of textual self-consciousness, if we can call it that, necessary for metafiction. In other words, the text is reflecting on its own operations in a kind of mimicry of our own self-consciousness. That, in turn, is why some exercises in textual self-reflexivity can be cloying or trivial or merely cute, just as there are actual humans whose self-consciousness is employed in grandstanding or navel-gazing or staring in the bathroom mirror saying their name again and again. But when textual self-awareness implicates or is implicated by intellectual disability, then we are dealing not only with a different kind of formal textual experiment (where the narrative is "warped" and the dominant protocols of representation are "short-circuited" by a character or group of characters) but also with a degree of moral seriousness that is not to be found in ordinary fun-house metafiction. Just as intellectually disabled narrative opens a window onto a reimagining of the parameters of narrative as such, so too does intellectually disabled self-consciousness open a window onto a reinterpretation of self-consciousness as such. And when it does, readers should (if they are reading disability as disability) keep in mind the "ethical core" of disability, the omnipresent and overwhelming question of how intellectually disabled literary characters—even the most metafictional ones—compel us to think about our social relations with humans of all varieties and capacities.

I stress this point not because I find myself profoundly moved by *Foe* or *Don Quixote*; I do not. Rather, I want to try to counter, at least to some degree, the standard critical response to self-reflexive metafictional texts. Rabinowitz's reading of *Pale Fire* is exemplary, because it goes well beyond "I can't get into the characters," into "The distance between the actual audience and the narrative audience prevents me from getting into the characters"—and because this reading has a good deal of merit. *Pale Fire*, Rabinowitz suggests, "makes us more aware of the gap between authorial and narrative audience, and hence of the novel as art, as construct. It is thus difficult to get involved in *Pale Fire* as narrative audience, and for many readers, including myself, the book is generally unmoving, witty and brilliant as it may be" (139).

I understand this complaint. I have heard it many times, not only from my friends and students but from my wife. (I like to tell people that we met in a twentieth-century literature class in which her favorite writer was D. H. Lawrence and mine was either André Gide or Samuel Beckett. *How's that marriage gonna work*, one might wonder.)[10] And it is true that it is difficult to care about the fates of characters when one is continually reminded that their own creator is not fully committed to the project of soliciting your belief in their existence even within the frame of the narrative, as when the witty but relentlessly intrusive narrator of Beckett's *Murphy* advises his readers that "all the puppets in this book whinge sooner or later, except Murphy, who is not a puppet" (122). It is the rare reader who opens a new novel and says, "I hope this one has lots of playful multilingual puns, obscure literary allusions, and strange concordances—I love tracking those down." But perhaps there is more than one way to be moved by a piece of literature, and perhaps there are metafictional gambits that do invite emotional responses from readers. Judy Boone's letters, in *Curious Incident*, do at least two things: they serve, as I have argued, as the textual device by which Christopher is made aware of (and made capable of narrating) the real conditions of the narrative he inhabits. They also break your heart into little bits, should you have one. Nabokov does not aim for the same effect, though I do think it is worth mentioning that the heart of John Shade's poem concerns the suicide of his daughter, who is so physically unattractive that she is abandoned on an ill-conceived blind date and decides as a result to take her life. Somewhere in *Pale Fire*'s hall of mirrors is a grieving father (if he exists, which, as a literary character, he does not) writing,

> While children of her age
> Were cast as elves and fairies on the stage
> That *she'd* helped paint for the school pantomime,
> My gentle girl appeared as Mother Time,
> A bent charwoman with slop pail and a broom,
> And like a fool I sobbed in the men's room. (44)

But that's not where I want to place my chips, finally, on the subject of *Pale Fire*. I promised, at the conclusion of the previous section, a reading of *Pale Fire* that obtains for all possible scenarios and goes to the heart of why any writer would explore the infinite terrain of metafiction by way of the deployment of intellectual disability. That reading pivots on Kinbote's paean to the written word, and is worth contemplating both for itself and for its use as a key to reading even the most frivolous word games in *Pale Fire*:

> We are absurdly accustomed to the miracle of a few written signs being able to contain immortal imagery, involutions of thought, new worlds with live people, speaking, weeping, laughing. We take it for granted so simply that in a sense, by the very act of brutish routine acceptance, we undo the work of the ages, the history of the gradual elaboration of poetical description and construction, from the tree-man to Browning, from the caveman to Keats. What if we awake one day, all of us, and find ourselves utterly unable to read? I wish you to gasp not only at what you read but at the miracle of its being readable (so I used to tell my students). (289)

This is a close analogue to, or perhaps a Zemblan translation of, Viktor Shklovsky's treatment of "habitualization":

> And so life is reckoned as nothing. Habitualization devours works, clothes, furniture, one's wife, and the fear of war. . . . And art exists that one may recover the sensation of life; it exists to make one feel things, to make the stone stony. The purpose of art is to impart the sensation of things as they are perceived and not as they are known. The technique of art is to make objects "unfamiliar," to make forms difficult, to increase the difficulty and length of perception because the process of perception is an aesthetic end in itself and must be prolonged. (12)

It is worth spelling out, letter by letter, why this is important, and why it is important to self-reflexive texts that involve intellectual disability.

Some years ago I took a deep breath and taught *Pale Fire* to undergraduates. I did so with much preparation, titling a senior seminar "Stranger Than Fiction" and warning unsuspecting students repeatedly that they would be reading things like *The Confidence-Man* and Richard Powers's *Prisoner's Dilemma*. By the time they got to *Pale Fire*, they were as accustomed to high-tech textual shenanigans as they could be—or so I believed. One day it occurred to me to ask how many of them had read Kinbote's foreword to the volume. My heart sank: of the fifteen, only two. "We thought it was just an introduction," said the other thirteen. "We thought the book started with the poem."

Very well, then. In my sorrow and dismay, I upped the ante. "And how many of you read the index?"

Blank stares. *There is an index*?

Yes there is, I told them, flipping to it. *And it is hilarious.* How many you have seen the *Airplane!* and *Naked Gun* series? (Almost all.) And you know to stick around for the credits, which are full of gags and in-jokes, right? (Right.) Well, turn to page 311, just at random, and read this:

> *Odon*, pseudonym of Donald O'Donnell, b. 1915, world-famous actor and Zemblan patriot; learns from K. about secret passage but has to leave for theater, *130*; drives K. from theater to foot of Mt. Mandevil, *149*; meets K. near sea cave and escapes with him in motorboat, *ibid.*; directs cinema picture in Paris, *171*; stays with Lavender in Lex, *408*; ought not to marry that blubber-lipped cinemactress, with untidy hair, *691*; see also O'Donnell, Sylvia.

The last item about the blubber-lipped cinemactress breaks the frame, serving not as an index item but as a warning to Odon from the misogynist Kinbote himself. And this is not even close to being the silliest item in the index; the entry on *Kinbote, Charles, Dr.*, is full of howlers.

But, but, but, my students cried, how were we to know we were supposed to read the foreword and the index?

Let me put it this way, I explained in a passionate yet (I hope) not terribly loud voice: when you pass over parts of the text, assuming they are of no account, you give in to brutish routine acceptance, you undo the work of the ages, the history of the gradual elaboration of poetical description and construction, from the treeman to Browning, from the caveman to Keats. You assume that some of the words are just filler. You fail to be astonished at what written language is, and what it can do. You miss the fine detail of a mirror signed by Sudarg of Bokay, you miss the little variations in the glitches of *Foe* and *Martian Time-Slip . . . all because you are not paying attention.* And so life is reckoned as nothing. Your inattention devours works, clothes, furniture, your boyfriends and girlfriends, and the fear of war. Nabokov was testing you to see whether you were reading carefully, and you failed. You let him down. *That* is why you read every word.

Most people are nearly blind, wrote Mark Haddon in his text-about-texts, and he was right. *Pale Fire* deploys intellectual disability in the service of proliferating possible novels, but it also deploys intellectual disability as an invitation to the kind of hyperattentiveness Christopher brings to every personal and textual encounter. Like Kingston's increasingly intellectually and narratively disabled Moon Orchid saying the spiders are spinning with legs intertwined and beating the eggs electrically, Nabokov's Kinbote is himself a vehicle for the renewal of perception, an exemplar of the capacity for literature to estrange, to make objects unfamiliar, to render people imaginable, and to displace the "normate" in every aspect of life. When you think about it that way—and you should—perhaps it becomes possible to see the value of, and even to become emotionally invested in, self-reflexive and metafictional renderings of intellectual disability.

Conclusion

Minds

In the spring of 2013, in the middle of a graduate seminar in which my students and I were working out many of the questions I have tried to pose here, suddenly a curious incident happened.

I was discussing chapters 2 and 3 of Lisa Zunshine's *Why We Read Fiction*. I was doing so for two reasons: one, to establish her unfortunate reliance on Simon Baron-Cohen, right down to her acceptance of his description of autism as the "most severe of all childhood *psychiatric conditions*" (qtd. at 7; emphasis added), a phrase that would not have looked at all out of place in *Martian Time-Slip*. Two, to establish what I took to be the key opening move in her argument about fiction and Theory of Mind, namely, that where there is Theory of Mind there will be novels, and where there are novels there is Theory of Mind: "The novel, in particular, is implicated with our mind-reading ability to such a degree that I do not think myself in danger of overstating anything when I say that in its currently familiar shape it exists because we are creatures with ToM" (10). (Theory of Mind is badly named, by the way—it proposes no theory of mind. It merely indicates that our minds are aware of other people's minds, and that therefore we recognize that other people have intentions, including the intention to tell us things that are not true.) Zunshine does not explain why, if we have had Theory of Mind for tens of thousands of years, the novel in its currently familiar shape (whatever that might be, from Austen to Robbe-Grillet) took so long to appear on our bio-cultural landscape; but she does explain why we have only recently begun to speak of Theory of Mind:

> Why do we need this newfangled concept of mind-reading, or ToM, to explain what appears so obvious? Our ability to interpret the behavior of people in terms of their underlying states of mind seems to be such an integral part of what we are as human beings that we could be understandably reluctant to dignify it with fancy terms and elevate it into a separate object of study. One reason that ToM has received the sustained attention of cognitive psychologists over the last twenty years is that they have come across people whose ability to "see bodies as animated by minds" is drastically impaired—people with autism. By studying autism and a related constellation of cognitive deficits (such as Asperger syndrome), cognitive scientists began to appreciate our mind-reading ability as a special cognitive endowment, structuring our everyday communication and cultural representations. (7)

Moments like these, I told my students, are why deconstruction was invented. The argument here (I will focus first on its form rather than its content) is that *we know we have Theory of Mind because some people don't*. In other words, the existence of X is predicated on the not-X; the exceptional condition becomes the condition for the not-exceptional. Deconstruction was particularly keen at finding and overturning these figure/ground relationships, and was properly suspicious of binary arrangements that involved one privileged term and one abjected term. So, I argued, Zunshine is adducing autism here only to cast it aside and get to the important stuff, namely, the way novels provide workouts for our brains, with only a drive-by pair of paragraphs on *Curious Incident* that (a) mention Christopher's distaste for "proper novels" but do not stop to ask what novel Christopher is citing as "proper" or why that might be important, and (b) conclude by saying, "Still, as a novel authored by a child with a compromised Theory of Mind (even if this child is himself a fictional character), *Curious Incident* is a much-needed reminder about the complexity of the issues involved in the relationship between autism and storytelling" (12). I do not think myself in danger of overstating anything when I say that this is a serious underreading of *Curious Incident*.

At this point, however, one of my students looked up from the seminar table in bewilderment. "I don't have any of this," she said, clearly lost in the depths of some horrible graduate-student nightmare in which one's text turns to gubbish before one's eyes.

"I'm sorry?" I replied, equally bewildered. The other eleven students all had print copies of Zunshine's book, and were following along without any problem. This student was reading a Kindle version of the book—in which there were no references to autism. Zunshine had stripped out all the passages mentioning autism, and had added an explanatory footnote in their place: "The original edition of this book contained a discussion of the implications for research on autism and Theory of Mind for the study of literature. I have eliminated this discussion from the present edition because given what I am learning about autism, I am now reluctant to make any generalizations about autism and fiction."

Zunshine's theory of Theory of Mind is still deeply problematic, for reasons I will elaborate, but in disability studies as in life, I think we should take our victories where we find them. Just a few months before my seminar discussion, at the 2013 convention of the Modern Language Association, Zunshine had given a bracingly self-critical paper titled "Real Mindblindness, or, I Was Wrong." (I believe it may have been the first paper in the history of the MLA since 1884 to bear that subtitle.) Her argument was precisely the one I wish Vermeule had made in her discussion of "situational" mindblindness— namely, that the attribution of mindblindness to people with autism is itself an example of misreading minds, an instance of neurotypical mindblindness: "It is the neurotypical observer who is 'mindblind' (i.e., incapable of reading the other person's mind) yet the label of mindblindness or 'impaired' theory of mind is firmly attached to the individual exhibiting the unconventional behavior." Zunshine's change of mind was induced partly by autistic writers such as Tito Mukhopadhyay, Donna Williams, and Dawn Prince, and partly by researchers such as Douglas Biklen (*Autism and the Myth of the Person Alone*) and Ralph Savarese (*Reasonable People*), whose adopted son DJ is nonverbal yet capable of writing astonishing work that shatters stereotypes about people with autism. In a passage cited by Zunshine, DJ Savarese offers advice to people who might have trouble interpreting his intentions:

> First, ignore my involuntary gestures, including my signs for "done" and "break." They fearfully hear years of negative fear and try to keep me locked into a cycle of autonomic impulses. Remember these gestures are not voluntary. They are just my body's way of responding to stimuli. If you respond to them as meaningful, they fearfully rev my heart more, but if you wait patiently and wordlessly, you free me to finally respond voluntarily. Once I've freed my body to respond, I can skip over the autonomic responses and give faster motor replies as the conversation continues.

Zunshine's paper concludes that "my argument was not affected in the least" by the excision of the discussion of autism in *Why We Read*

Fiction. "At this point," Zunshine insists, "references to autism in cognitive literary criticism are gratuitous. We lose nothing by leaving them behind."

The good news is that chapter 3 of Zunshine's book, "Theory of Mind, Autism, and Fiction: Three Caveats," no longer exists in the Kindle version (I think it should be marked by a blank chapter or a black page, à la *Tristram Shandy*). The bad news is that Zunshine continues to rely heavily on Theory of Mind, and in her follow-up book, *Getting Inside Your Head*, she expands her argument to cover all of human culture, from novels to films and plays and musicals and paintings and reality shows. All the world's a Theory of Mind stage, except that the world we have created includes millions of actual stages, where actors embody the principle that all the world's a (self-reflexive) stage. Our culture, Zunshine writes, is "*a culture of greedy mind readers*" (11) that relentlessly invents scenes of "*embodied transparency*" (23) in which characters are briefly readable to each other and/or to us. In such scenes, we become able—or we are led to think we are able—to translate body language into a statement of intent: "That body, by virtue of being the object of our theory of mind's obsessive attention, is a *tremendously valuable and, as such, potentially misleading* source of information about the person's mental state" (14–15). It is potentially misleading, that is, because we can always feign a look, a posture, an expression, or a gesture: "We end up *performing our bodies* . . . to shape other people's perceptions of our mental states" (15). Scenes of embodied transparency, then, delight us because they fulfill the brain's need to decode social signals:

> Instances of embodied transparency offer us something that we hold at a premium in our everyday life and never get much of: the experience of perfect access to other people's minds in complex social situations. As such, they must be immensely flattering to our theory-of-mind ad-

aptations, which evolved to read minds through bodies but have to constantly contend with the possibility of misreading and resulting social failure. (23)

As in *Why We Read Fiction*, Zunshine's work does highlight some interesting features of narrative—brief moments when characters are rendered legible at moments of contemplation, anger, or high drama. The moments must be brief, Zunshine argues, because only social sadists try to render people legible for long periods, usually by means of torture or emotional cruelty.

And why do we need to experience such fleeting scenes in fictional representational forms? Zunshine offers a couple of possibilities: "Does consuming embodied transparency on the page, onstage, and on screen sharpen our appetite for it in our everyday life? Do we start perceiving people around us as more transparent than they are? Or do we get addicted to shows and stories that offer us a steady supply of readable bodies?" (28). Zunshine's money is (mostly) on the last of these, because that's where her theory of Theory of Mind pays the highest dividends: "It's only when we start thinking of mind reading as our most crucial and constant preoccupation (though not consciously so) as a social species that we can say that we like watching displays of emotion because they promise access to people's thoughts, feelings, and intentions, and we evolved to value such access tremendously" (120–21).

The problem is that when all you have is a Theory of Mind hammer, everything starts to look like a Theory of Mind nail. In *Why We Read Fiction*, the novel has its "currently familiar shape" because we are creatures with Theory of Mind; in *Getting Inside Your Head*, pretty much everything has its currently familiar shape for the same reason. "Movies, of course," Zunshine writes, "*are* theory-of-mind writ large" (79)—apparently without exception. And one genre is Theory of Mind writ larger: "Because mock documentaries represent only a small segment of television programming, I feel justified in saying that they literally exist to cultivate moments of embodied transparency" (117). (I confess I do not understand the "because" here: if we value such moments so highly, wouldn't mock documentaries represent a *large* segment of television programming?) Art criticism turns out also to be all about Theory of Mind: "This is what art criticism does—it introduces more mental states into our perception of an artwork" (154). Even abstract, nonrepresentational art turns out to be all about Theory of Mind: "It is as if we approach each painting ready and eager to attribute states of mind, and if something prevents us from attributing them to the subjects of the painting, we turn with the same eagerness to the artist and start thinking about her mind, and if we can't do that, we begin to attribute mental states to ourselves" (150). So much for the possibility that in gazing at a painting, one might be looking at line, form, color, or texture. But the claim that I might be attributing mental states to myself in my contemplation of some monumental black painting by Richard Serra seems to be a last-ditch attempt to salvage a Theory of Mind reading of abstract art at the cost of understanding abstraction—and understanding art.

Eve Sedgwick, in a fascinating essay contrasting Theory of Mind with Silvan Tomkins's "affect theory" (which she was instrumental in bringing to bear on literary and cultural studies), suggests that the problems with Theory of Mind, as a theory, go still deeper than this.[1] It is not merely that its overapplication, as in *Getting Inside Your Head*, can be brutally reductive; it is also that the theory itself is something like an on/off switch. Sedgwick notes, rightly, that in *Why We Read Fiction*, Zunshine concentrates largely on unreliable narrators and on cognitively complex scenes in the work of Virginia Woolf or Henry James in which readers are required, if they are to navigate the text successfully, to determine what character A thinks about character

B's worry that character C is insufficiently aware that character D has a very low opinion of character E. "Even though I take Zunshine's point that a workout with five or six layers of narrative irony can be an exhilarating thing," Sedgwick writes,

> I'm dismayed by how much the bulk of her readings have to depend on that rackety warhorse of high-school English classes, the Unreliable Narrator. She suggests that by mastering Theory of Mind, with the attendant disciplines of neurobiology and human evolution, we can learn to ponder mysteries such as "How do we know Henry James's governess isn't a delusional head case?" and "What if that erudite Professor Kinbote is just an evil queen?" . . . [T]he problem is that her readings really do *have to* cleave to the most reductive version of the Unreliable Narrator problematic. The constraint lies in Theory of Mind itself. (150)

This is something of a disappointment for Sedgwick, who, by her own account, turned to Theory of Mind because it seemed to offer a way into the problem sketched out in Axiom 1 of *Epistemology of the Closet*, namely, "people are different from each other" (22). In acknowledging that other people have other minds, the theory of Theory of Mind would seem to enable the kind of radical individuation I have pursued in this study. But it turns out quite otherwise, not only for our understanding of other minds but also for the application of that understanding to the reading of literature:

> After all, the reason one's heart sinks when students reach for the Unreliable Narrator is that that heuristic persists in addressing even the most complex narrative with a single, all too flattening, yes-or-no question: reliable or not reliable? As though a narrator or character who's not certifiable, vicious, or systematically mendacious is thereby

reliable. But then as though "reliable" itself is a single thing to be, a single kind of normative transparency or relationality. But if that is assumed, it would essentially undo the space for individual difference that's supposed to be secured by achieving Theory of Mind in the first place. (150)

Sedgwick then proceeds to show, by way of a reading of Proust, that "Theory of Mind is in no degree a purely cognitive issue" (154), and then, by way of an engagement with autistic writers who reject the attribution of mindblindness to them, to offer six suggestions for reconceptualizing theories of mind, the first two of which run as follows:

1. Don't work toward, or depend on the model of, development of a single, normative outcome—with differences from that outcome analyzed in terms of deficiency or at best detour.
2. Instead, find ways of discerning and describing a variety of outcomes, qualitatively and phenomenologically distinct; not understood in terms of a preimagined evolutionary teleology, but instead in terms of a diversity of potentials. Only the latter mode can be relevant to a range of possible futures and to the rules of contingency and plurality that remain at the center of evolutionary process. (159–60)

I focus on these two programmatic conclusions not only because I have attempted to follow them here, but because they point to something more pernicious lurking in the world of literary Darwinism—its attempt to reinstall universal, species-wide, radically transhistorical human norms. With a vengeance.

Zunshine is by no means the worst offender in this respect. On the contrary, I believe there is an important difference between cognitive literary studies (in Zunshine's work) and evocriticism/literary Darwinism (in the work of Joseph Carroll, Brian Boyd, and the late Denis Dutton), and that Zunshine's use of Theory of Mind is relatively benign. Though it is badly overextended in *Getting Inside Your Head*, in *Why We Read Fiction* it serves as an analogue to Wolfgang Iser's theory of reader response—an implied reader with Theory of Mind, if you will, for Zunshine's arguments are all about how literary texts make specific cognitive demands on the figure once known in reader-response narratology as the "implied reader" (Iser) or the "narratee" (Gerald Prince). In the work of the evocritics/literary Darwinists, by contrast, we find an antipathy to individuation that is matched only by an antipathy to textual interpretation—not a promising combination for a fledgling school of literary criticism. But despite her significant differences from evocritics, Zunshine's treatment of Steven Pinker, at the close of the first section of *We Why Read Fiction*, is far too kind—and this excess of kindness has serious implications not only for how one reads modernist and experimental narratives but also for the kind of "interdisciplinarity" imagined by advocates of cognitive and evolutionary literary studies.

Zunshine's chapter is titled "Woolf, Pinker, and the Project of Interdisciplinarity," so the stakes are quite clear. I will cite the opening of the chapter at some length:

> Challenging as it may be, Woolf's prose is so fundamentally rooted in our cognitive capacities that I am compelled to qualify an argument advanced recently by Steven Pinker in his remarkable and provocative *Blank Slate*. Pinker sees Woolf as having inaugurated an aesthetic movement whose "philosophy did not acknowledge the ways in which it was appealing to human pleasure." Although he admits that "modernism comprises many styles and artists . . . not [all of which] rejected beauty and other human sensibilities" and that modernist "fiction and

poetry offered invigorating intellectual workouts," here is what he has
to say about modernism as a whole and Woolf in particular:

> The giveaway [explanation for the current crisis in the arts and
> humanities] may be found in a famous statement from Vir-
> ginia Woolf: "[On] or about December 1910, human [character]
> changed." She was referring to the new philosophy of modern-
> ism that would dominate the elite arts and criticism for much of
> the twentieth century, and whose denial of human nature was
> carried over with a vengeance to postmodernism, which seized
> control in later decades. . . . Modernism certainly proceeded *as
> if* human nature had changed. All the tricks that artists had used
> for millennia to please the human palate were cast aside. . . . In
> literature, omniscient narration, structured plots, the orderly in-
> troduction of characters, and general readability were replaced
> by a stream of consciousness, events presented out of order, baf-
> fling characters and causal sequences, subjective and disjointed
> narration, and difficult prose. (404, 409–10)

As literary critics, we have several ways of responding to Pinker's
claims about Woolf. We can hope, together with a representative of
The Publications of the Modern Language Association [*sic*], that not
"many students, teachers, theorists, and critics of literature will take
[him] seriously as an authority on literature or the aesthetics more
generally, especially since he misrepresents both Woolf and modernism." At first sight, this is a comfortable stance. It assumes a certain
cultural detachment of literary studies and implies that cognitive scientists should just leave literature alone, acknowledging it as an exclusive playing field for properly trained professionals—us. (40–41)

Zunshine proceeds to lament "our own relative interdisciplinary
timidity" (43)—relative to that of cognitive scientists, that is—and
urge that we make a "good-faith effort to meet Pinker halfway" (44).

But what can this possibly mean? Pinker's position is that modernism constitutes a violation of human nature, and he even misquotes Woolf on "human character" (Pinker had construed Woolf's line as "on or about December 1910, human nature changed," and Zunshine dutifully corrected the error).² Is the "halfway" point a position that modernism constitutes only a partial violation of human nature? As for whether literary critics are being narrowly professionalist in rejecting Pinker's account: let us find some analogy for the strange way we are being hailed here. For what are physicists supposed to do, for example, when someone outside their field complains that quantum theory violates common sense and cuts the sciences off from ordinary people who know that what goes up must come down? Because, truth be told, quantum theory is even weirder than modernist art and literature, and even fewer people understand it. That, clearly, is where the discipline of physics took a wrong turn, turning its back on what had worked for millennia.

The point, clearly, is that Pinker doesn't care for proper novels like *The Waves*. To her credit, Zunshine does, and her work touches on relatively challenging twentieth-century fare such as *Mrs. Dalloway* and *Lolita*.³ But Pinker's abreaction to the last hundred years of art and literature has a counterpart in evocriticism's intense antipathy to literary theory, which sometimes sounds like a longing for a sudden news flash—*This just in, sign not arbitrary after all*. (As Boyd puts it, "Joseph Carroll has long combated the indeterminacy of meaning" [64]. I presume this means that Carroll has won, and meanings will henceforth be stable, as Ahab had desired.) Though Pinker himself does not subscribe to the notion that art is an evolutionary adaptation, that aversion to modernism and to critical theory is shared by Carroll, Boyd, and Dutton, who have placed all their chips on the adaptationist thesis. Storytelling has a demonstrable survival value. It is therefore vitally important to us as a species (as long as it isn't too weird and/or experimental and/or theoretical or even disabled, which would lead it to violate human nature), and therefore, an interdisciplinary form of literary criticism that strives for "consilience" (in E. O. Wilson's coinage) will highlight the centrality of narrative to our lives and thereby save the humanities from themselves.

The problem with this adaptationist argument is that it can't be demonstrated; it can only be taken on faith. Humans might very well be hardwired for storytelling, at least over the last thirty or forty thousand years, when we received whatever cognitive upgrades were necessary to allow us to draw on caves and try to entertain and/or edify and/or bamboozle each other by making things up. Peter Brooks would apparently agree, to gauge by the passage with which I opened this book, and his example suggests that one can readily acknowledge the ubiquity of storytelling among humans without spinning any Just So stories about its origins. And yet Just So stories are precisely, for Dutton, what Darwinism requires: "Thoroughgoing Darwinism makes a specific demand: nothing can be proposed as an adaptive function of fiction unless it explains how the human appetite for fictional narratives acted to increase, however marginally, the chances of our Pleistocene forebears surviving and procreating" (109–10). It is only a slight exaggeration to say that Dutton's position, like that of Carroll, can be paraphrased as *The elephant has a long trunk, and the giraffe has a long neck, and humans tell stories, and thus I have refuted Judith Butler.* As Jonathan Kramnick pointed out in a devastating review of the field, "Against Literary Darwinism," "Once this move has been taken, literary Darwinism can begin its cleaning out of the stables of the humanities. Adaptationism is therefore the underlying rationale and opening gambit" (322).[4]

But what part of storytelling served to get us through the Pleistocene, one wonders. In Kramnick's follow-up reply to Carroll, Boyd et al.'s responses to the original essay, the answer is whatever part you feel like stressing:

> There is (again) no way to adjudicate between Carroll's belief that literature provides an emotional skein to brute existence and Dutton's that literature was useful for counterfactual role playing or Vermeule and Dutton's that literary language was a kind of courtship ornament or Boyd's that stories and other art forms hold our attention and so "make the most of the brain's plasticity" (Boyd 94). Each is merely one belief asserted against another. (446–47)

For that matter, there is no evidence that storytelling *in general* conferred an evolutionary advantage on us, as opposed to some combination of traits and proclivities that go into storytelling, as Kramnick argues in his initial essay: "It might accompany features of mind that do serve some advantage—modal syntax, memory, imagining objects and events not immediately present—and yet still be a *further fact*, subject to more local and historical constraints, like writing and literacy, for example" (332).

Boyd, for his part, opens *On the Origin of Stories*—with its obvious nod to Darwin in the title—by assuring his fellow humanists that he is not a genetic reductionist. As he puts it, "We should see genes less as constraints than as enablers," just as "we should see genes not as deniers of the role of the environment but as devices for extracting information *from* the environment" (24). Boyd acknowledges that "those uneasy about applying evolution to human behavior often assume that doing so must require stressing selfishness and competition at the expense of altruism and cooperation," but notes that it ain't necessarily so: "[Richard] Dawkins points out that he could with equal validity, though with less impact, have called his famous first book not *The Selfish Gene* but *The Cooperative Gene*" (26). That's nice to know after all these years, now that three decades of popular-science enthusiasts have convinced themselves that Nature herself speaks in the language of Ayn Rand. One hopes the word will get around.

Notably, Boyd shares Pinker's antipathy to environmental explanations for human behavior, and (relatedly) his taste for concocting social-constructionist straw-humanists who apparently believe that human beings are infinitely malleable. Boyd thereby works himself into a nasty and unnecessary self-contradiction in his first chapter, where he argues that "the cultural constructionist's view of the mind as a blank slate is 'a dictator's dream' [quoting Steven Pinker]," for "if we were entirely socially constructed, our 'society' could mold us into slaves and masters, and there would be no reason to object" (26–27). This is a shallow conception of social constructionism, in which saying that "X is socially constructed" is tantamount to saying that "X can be changed at will." But what makes Boyd's critique so unfortunate (and self-contradictory) is that he immediately proceeds to insist that, unlike social constructionism, "an evolutionary view allows for *informed* social change": "Owen Jones," he writes, "compares the law to a lever to change human behavior, and an informed knowledge of human nature to the fulcrum the lever needs to exert its force" (27). If this lever-fulcrum apparatus really works, how is this evolutionary view *not* a dictator's dream?

But the really important thing here for Boyd is (of course) the origin of stories. Like the other evocritics, Boyd is convinced that art is good for us (quite apart from allowing us to survive all these years), in that it hones and enhances those functions of mind that in turn enhance our capacity for social interaction and exploration:

> Art develops in us habits of imaginative exploration, so that we take the world not as closed and given, but open and to be shaped on our own terms. . . . By refining and strengthening our sociality, by making

us readier to use the resources of the imagination, and by raising our confidence in shaping life on our own terms, art fundamentally alters our relation to the world. The survival consequences may be difficult to tabulate, but they are profound. We have long felt that art matters to us. It does, objectively as well as subjectively. By focusing our attention away from the given to a world of shared, humanly created possibility, art makes all the difference. (124–25)

I think it would be a mistake for humanists to dismiss this line of thought out of hand. This is rousing stuff; it not merely reassures us that all our museum-brochure rhetoric is telling the truth, but also, and more importantly, confirms that Friedrich Schiller was right to propose, in *On the Aesthetic Education of Man*, that humans possess a "play-drive" that leads us to create and be amazed by art: "For, to declare it once and for all, Man plays only when he is in the full sense of the word a man, and *he is only wholly Man when he is playing*. This proposition . . . will, I promise you, support the whole fabric of aesthetic art, and the still more difficult art of living" (80). It is no slight to Boyd to say that *On the Origin of Stories* sometimes reads like Schiller combined with a few graduate courses in neuroscience. Whether one prefers to say, with Emily Dickinson, "If I feel physically as if the top of my head were taken off, I know that is poetry," or, with Boyd, "Neurons in the substantia nigra and the ventral tegmental areas of the brain secrete dopamine in reaction to the surprising but not to the expected" (184) is merely a matter of taste.

The second half of the book, however, turns out to be a profound disappointment. It bears the subtitle "From Zeus to Seuss," lending the section a kind of alpha-to-omega sweep that suggests it practically covers everything worth covering about literature.[5] Boyd opens by assuring readers that "a biocultural approach to literature simply requires that we take seriously that evolution has powerfully shaped not just our bodies but also our minds and behavior" (210). This much is incontrovertible; but Boyd's application of the principle has two overwhelming weaknesses. The first is that the resulting readings of *The Odyssey* and *Horton Hears a Who* don't appear to be worth the journey. Much of Boyd's approach consists of explaining how Homer and Dr. Seuss managed to win and keep our attention, and Boyd castigates contemporary literary criticism for failing to attend to this important matter. But might it not be that "Homer organized the poem in this way so as to win and keep your attention" is the kind of thing that, in literary criticism, literally goes without saying? (I will return to this point a bit later on.) Similarly, readers have known for almost three millennia that Odysseus is one crafty fellow, and one index of his craftiness is that he does not act on impulse; even when he's trapped in a cave with a one-eyed giant eating his men, he remains reflective and comes up with a well-considered plan. Boyd explains precisely what this means in neurological terms: "Rapid-fire reactions have to be inhibited (in the orbitofrontal cortex) so that there is time to formulate and assess new options (in the dorsolateral cortex) before acting on them" (258). Personally, I am tremendously pleased that my species has gotten to the point at which it understands things like this in such a minute and precise way. But how much is added to the history of criticism, finally, by the realization that Odysseus was doing his crafty plotting in his dorsolateral cortex?[6]

This is a real and not a rhetorical question. Boyd closes *On the Origin of Stories* by remarking that "evocriticism" will have to make its way by devising compelling and convincing readings of works of literature, attending not only to the universal features of human minds but also to the cultural and historical particularities of time and place. On one hand, this school of criticism will provide a desperately needed justification for literary study: "If storytelling sharpens our social cognition, prompts us to reconsider human experience, and spurs our creativity in the way that comes most naturally to us"—as it surely does—"then literary studies need not apologize" (384). On the other hand, evocriticism comes bearing not only a rationale but also a sword: as Boyd remarks time and again, the enemy to be vanquished is Theory, "which cuts literature off from life by emphasizing human thought and ideas as the product of only language, convention, and ideology—although Theory then tries to compensate for severing literature from three-dimensional life by insisting that it is always political or ideological" (385).

It is odd, to say the least, for a literary critic to suggest that stressing "language, convention, and ideology" somehow cuts one off from "life" (one would have imagined that these were aspects of human social life, and important ones too—things that developed because of the evolution of our brains).[7] It is similarly strange for someone to claim that "a fine work of art not only expresses creativity but also inspires it in those who enjoy it" (376–77) but fail to consider that "theoretical" readings of language and literature caught on in the 1970s and 1980s because they were, back in the day, compelling and creative. Everyone who, like Boyd, believes that Alan Sokal killed Theory dead in 1996 really should go back and read Barbara Johnson on Melville's *Billy Budd* or Paul de Man on the famous rhetorical (or is it real?) question that closes Yeats's "Among School Children."[8] As for myself, even though I've never been a card-carrying deconstructionist, I was fascinated by those readings when I first encountered them because they taught me that Melville's novella was even more extraordinary than I'd thought, and that when you're trying to determine whether a question is real or rhetorical, even an utterance like "eh, what's the difference?" can open onto a hall of mirrors. Boyd never stops to consider that maybe, just maybe, the clever human minds responsible for literature are the same clever human minds responsible for literary theory; if he had, he might have been able to say, more plausibly, that Theory started (as do all our endeavors) in the impulse to play and create, and became routine and stultifying only after many weary iterations. At which point, after the 350th New Historicist reading of *The Tempest*, neurons in the substantia nigra and ventral tegmental areas of the brain stopped secreting dopamine, and people decided to do something else instead.

More importantly, Boyd is exceptionally reluctant to give culture and history their due—as most humanists understand these things. He scoffs, for example, at the idea that romantic love was invented at some point in the twelfth century, because "cross-cultural, neurological, and cross-species studies have demonstrated the workings of romantic love across societies and even species" (341). This just won't wash, in the humanities *or* in the sciences. "Romantic love" in the sense used by contemporary humanists does not mean "mammals doing it like mammals"; it refers to the conventions of courtly love, which were indeed invented in the European Middle Ages, and cannot be found in ancient literatures or cultures. Those conventions are culturally and historically specific variations on our underlying (and polymorphous) biological imperatives, just as the institution of the $25,000 wedding is specific to our own addled time and place. Nothing about the evolutionary record, from amoebas to *Homo sapiens sapiens*, is denied or contravened in acknowledging this.

It is a shame that a branch of criticism purportedly devoted to explaining our abiding love for storytelling turns out to be so sweepingly dismissive of so much of the intellectual traditions humans have devised for the study of human cultures. Even worse, this branch of criticism, in its hostility to every other school of criticism, seems to have no interest in getting into the grainy textual details of individual stories—or the various interpretive disputes about those stories— that make up so much of the work of literary criticism. Once you have decided that all art and storytelling is an evolutionary adaptation that got us through the Pleistocene, it appears, you have said everything worth saying, and the only task remaining is to take other critics to task for not remarking that storytellers have devised a variety of ways to win and hold our attention. Nor is it clear that the insights vouchsafed to us by evocriticism couldn't have been arrived at without evocriticism. In *The Storytelling Animal*, for instance, Jonathan Gottschall insists that fiction has a generally moral effect on us, creating communities not unlike those formed by religious belief, which in turn rests on the power of stories. But why is this (hopeful if not naive) understanding of literature any better than that proposed by Matthew Arnold long before the advent of neuroscience? Likewise, Gottschall rightly suggests that humans need a sense of order and coherence that only narrative can provide. But why is this understanding of narrative any better than that proposed by Kermode in *The Sense of an Ending*?

But finally, the most remarkable and disturbing problem with evocriticism is that its understanding of stories doesn't have anything to say about the difference between oral and written literature, or literature and visual media. (And though Zunshine's work has none of the evocritics' adaptationist commitments, *Getting Inside Your Head* is, as we have seen, aggressively indifferent to such concerns as well.) This is not an oversight. As Kramnick points out, "The adaptation thesis speaks to dimensions of literary competence that may be said to be very old, present in the notional prehistory of the human species, prior to writing, literacy, or any work with which we are familiar" (326).[9] At this reach, evocriticism is not merely a question of spanning Zeus to Seuss. It proposes that storytelling is important because it helped us fend off predators and manage a series of Ice Ages, and that nothing about the evolution of storytelling since its origin is as important as that. What makes this claim especially weird is that in

2007 a practicing neuroscientist (i.e., a real scientist, not a literary critic with a secondary interest in evolution and neuroscience) wrote a book about the importance of the invention of writing, a book that one would think might be of some interest to people who claim to be interested in evolution and narrative—people who believe, as Gottschall does, that fiction works by "literally rewiring our brains" (63). That book was Maryanne Wolf's *Proust and the Squid*, and it makes a persuasive and detailed case for the way the invention of writing (as opposed to the general invention of lying and storytelling) rewired our brains. To date, not a single evocritic has given Wolf's argument the time of day, precisely because it would require an attention to written language and historical specificity that is anathema to the project of literary Darwinism.

In *Comeuppance: Costly Signaling, Altruistic Punishment, and Other Biological Components of Fiction* (which, as its title suggests, is sympathetic to the project of reading literature in broadly evolutionary terms), William Flesch suggests that the hard-core literary Darwinists are, at bottom, hostile not only to literary theory but to certain kinds of textual interpretation more broadly. For Flesch, the evocritics fail to say anything particularly illuminating about individual literary works not only because they are committed to an ever-since-the-Pleistocene approach but also because they have surprisingly low expectations of literature itself:

> The people tempted to apply evolutionary psychology to the explanation of literature tend to be extremely reductive. . . . Although they would certainly not put it this way, they think they have good reasons to suppose that literature cannot be as subtle and as deep as the best literary criticism takes it to be, or rather they think there is no good reason to suppose that literature could be as subtle and deep as literary criticism claims. (1)

This sounds unlikely—seriously, there are professional literary critics who think that literature isn't all that?—but Boyd's work bears it out completely, arguing that "meaning" is epiphenomenal, a second-order effect that deserves lower priority than allegedly more pressing matters:

> Academic literary criticism tends to focus on meaning, on the *themes* of traditional critics or the *ideologies* of more recent ones. But works of art need to attract and arouse audiences before they "mean." Every detail of a work will affect the moment-by-moment attention it receives, but not necessarily a meaning abstracted from the story. Our minds can focus on only a few things at once. To hold an audience, in a world of competing demands on attention, an author needs to be an inventive intuitive psychologist. Yet criticism has tended to underplay the "mere" ability to arouse and hold attention. (232)

At this point, I think, it becomes clear that the interpretive shortcomings of literary Darwinisms are not bugs in the system; they are features of the system's design. For Boyd, attracting and arousing the attention of audiences is prior to any audience's understanding of "meaning," and the attraction-and-arousal mechanism is to be understood in (his version of) evolutionary terms. It does not have to be this way; Flesch, for instance, manages to devise a kind of Nussbaumian *Poetic Justice*-plus-neuroscience argument about why we like to see punishment meted out to rapscallions, mountebanks, and assorted social cheaters, and he focuses almost exclusively on texts by Dickens and Shakespeare in which justice is or is not done. Flesch generously exempts Zunshine from his indictment of evocriticism, and rightly so; however, in raising the question of justice and "altruistic punishment" (also known as comeuppance), Flesch points to something that will turn out to be devastating for Zunshine's *Getting Inside Your Head* (which was published five years after *Comeuppance*).

Recall that in *Why We Read Fiction*, Zunshine had claimed that the novel "in its currently familiar shape" arose because of Theory of Mind. *Getting Inside Your Head* effectively undermines that argument by claiming that *all* human cultural productions arose because of Theory of Mind. If that is the case, and if there is nothing to be said about any specific cultural production other than "this too is the product of Theory of Mind," or (in Boyd's version) "this too required its creator to attract and hold our attention," why should my argument in this book have anything to do with evocriticism and its second cousin, cognitive literary criticism? My sense is that a theory of Theory of Mind is potentially relevant to a study of intellectual disability in fiction, but there is a larger question at stake here as well, and it has to do with (of all things) justice. Zunshine is right to think that scenes of embodied transparency, in which we can divine the mental states of others, are important elements of fiction. But surely they are not the only, or even necessarily the primary, reason that humans create and consume narratives. Sometimes, we ask other questions: What happens to the characters, and is what happens to them right and just? (Mental states may be part of this question, but the abstract question of justice is not.) What kind of world is being created in this fiction? If it is prose narrative, what is the language like? If it is film or visual art, what does it look like?

In her reading of the film *Quiz Show*, Zunshine unwittingly offers a handy example of how the Theory of Mind approach can miss the moral forest for the cognitive trees: "The quiz shows promised one kind of cognitive management and delivered another—that was their real 'scandal'" (100). This makes sense only if you believe that the contestants on *Twenty-One* and *Tic-Tac-Dough* were really performing embodied transparency, whereupon you feel betrayed when you realize that their reactions were scripted. If you're a reader like Zunshine, you watch game shows to see emotions, and you want to see real ones. But surely the real scandal of the quiz shows, for most people, was *not* that they promised one kind of cognitive management and delivered another. The real scandal is that they purported to show real competition but did not. We thought we were watching a fair contest; we didn't know the entire game was rigged. Somehow, that seems more important than the cognitive benefits I might have derived from seeing how contestants behaved in the thrill of victory or the agony of defeat.

At a key moment in *Getting Inside Your Head*, Zunshine brushes off alternate ways of perceiving art, such as the possibility that representations of women might have something to do with ideas about sexuality: "A hypothesis that a given group of paintings featuring women reflects its time's anxiety about women's sexuality will be true about *any* group of paintings featuring women. It is thus *trivially* true because it does not predict anything about any specific painting or representational tradition" (176). It is a curious charge, since of course the same thing can be said of readings relying on Theory of Mind: they will be trivially true about any narrative that offers scenes of embodied transparency. But they will be irrelevant to forms of art, abstract or otherwise, that do not offer such scenes, and they will be indifferent to or determinedly clueless about questions of right and wrong—in quiz shows as on all the stages of the world.

* * *

I said in my introduction that my method here is formalist; yet no matter how formalist I try to be in my reading of literary works dealing with intellectual disability, it remains impossible to bracket out entirely the question of justice. Especially when we turn our attention to what, if anything, an intellectually disabled character knows about the narrative he or she inhabits, we are inevitably asking highly specific questions about specific texts, questions that are not well addressed by answers like "the author tried to win and hold your attention" but that can be broached, in a rudimentary way, by answers like "we are predisposed to be interested in what other people think, and in whether what happens to them is right and just." And as Frank Kermode would remind us, none of us knows where our (personal or collective) narrative trajectories might take us. It is one thing, therefore, to note that Steinbeck's Lennie Small is marked, from start to finish, by his inability to understand his own narrative and its (ultimately fatal) consequences, and to try to develop an argument from that observation; this is merely a matter of literary criticism. It is quite another thing to note that in Texas, an inmate can be legally executed, despite the Supreme Court's 2002 ruling on the unconstitutionality of capital punishment for people with intellectual disabilities, if he or she has a mental capacity that, in the determination of the court, exceeds Lennie's. That was the legal basis for the execution of Marvin Wilson in 2012, an execution whose rationale was strenuously criticized by Steinbeck's son Thomas and by the legal analyst Andrew Cohen, who noted that Wilson "could not handle money or navigate a phone book" and was "a man who sucked his thumb and could not always tell the difference between left and right, a man who, as a child, could not match his socks, tie his shoes or button his clothes."[10]

In the 2004 decision *Ex Parte Briseno*, the Texas Court of Criminal Appeals wrote,

> Most Texas citizens would agree that Steinbeck's Lennie should, by virtue of his lack of reasoning ability and adaptive skills, be exempt from execution. But does a consensus of Texas citizens agree that all persons who might legitimately qualify for assistance under the social services definition of mental retardation be exempt from an otherwise constitutional penalty?

Put another way, is there a national or Texas consensus that all of those persons whom the mental health profession might diagnose as meeting the criteria for mental retardation are automatically less morally culpable than those who just barely miss meeting those criteria? Is there, and should there be, a "mental retardation" bright-line exemption from our state's maximum statutory punishment?

The idea is a simple and utterly reprehensible one: the understanding of intellectual disability in fiction can be used as a device for exempting some people with intellectual disabilities from the Supreme Court decision in *Atkins v. Virginia*—and killing them.

As we saw in *Martian Time-Slip*, where narrative experiments with time and textual self-awareness were intertwined with discussions of genocide with regard to people with intellectual disability, the interpretive stakes are always high when the subject is intellectual disability, because the stakes are ultimately about who is and who is not determined to be "fully human," and what is to be done with those who (purportedly) fail to meet the prevailing performance criteria for being human. I have had moments, over the years of writing and thinking about this book, in which I have said to myself that I do not care whether this book has any impact on public policy or on the scales of social justice; it is a work of literary criticism, meant to continue and expand a conversation among a small group of specialists who practice the arts of advanced literacy. For that task, too, requires attention, just as scholars in history, philosophy, and the arts need to take more adequate account of the importance of disability to their fields. And yet in the course of my reading, I have found myself time and again in the position Ato Quayson marks out for himself at the end of *Aesthetic Nervousness*. After performing all his readings of the work of Samuel Beckett, Toni Morrison, Wole Soyinka, and J. M. Coetzee, Quayson finds himself contemplating the work of the Centre for Democratic Development in Ghana—specifically, his own 2006 lecture to mark the passage of Ghana's Persons with Disability Act. "I kept asking myself," Quayson writes, "both then and afterward: what is the relation between *Aesthetic Nervousness* and an occasion such as this, between a discussion of the representation of disability in literature and the condition of the lives of disabled persons on the streets of the city where I grew up?" (207–8).

To this question, Quayson first proposes an intermediary answer grounded in the protocols of textual analysis:

> It entails reading disability not as a discrete entity within the literary aesthetic domain, but as part of the totality of textual representation. In this totality, everything is linked to everything else such that in isolating a detail of disability for analysis we take it not merely as a particular detail, but as a threshold that opens up to other questions of a textual and also ethical kind. (208)

It is then a short distance—though it seems to entail a precipitous ratcheting-up of the stakes—to Quayson's final answer to the question, his conclusion that "our ultimate obligation as literary critics must be addressing the particularities of injustice of the world in which we live" (210). When it comes to disability—and, I would argue, intellectual disability *a fortiori*—even the most formalist readings are never strictly formalist: disability studies in literature might move beyond the analysis of individual bodies and minds, but its ultimate concern will always be centered on bodies and minds, and the nature of the social fabric that constitutes the relation between bodies and minds.

I have argued that if disability studies is going to have greater influence on the world of literary criticism, the degree of influence it can and should have, it needs to pay closer attention to the textuality of texts. But disability studies will never be *only* about the textuality of texts. The question of what Lennie knows about the narrative he inhabits is a formal question; it is also a social question. As I said in my opening pages, I hope that this book has made this argument so effectively that it has become obvious. And yet I remain thoroughly unconvinced that anything I have written in this book will have any effect on public policy or on the scales of social justice. I know, for instance, that it will not bring back Marvin Wilson, and that it does not provide any legal grounds for barring the execution of people like him in the future. But if, finally, I have convinced you that the study of intellectual disability is also the study of sociality; if I have convinced you that a disabled narrative or a fictional disability can change what you see and believe; if I have convinced you that every performance criterion for being human is pernicious; if I have convinced you that studying intellectual disability in literature is a worthwhile endeavor and that even so outlandish a novel as *Martian Time-Slip* has serious implications for addressing the injustice of the world in which we live—then I will have done all I can imagine doing in a book like this.

NOTES

INTRODUCTION

1 The film opens with a teenaged Magneto realizing his metal-bending powers as his parents are led off to Auschwitz. We move to the present, where the U.S. Senate is debating a bill that would require all mutants to wear identifying marks; Professor Xavier, in his wheelchair, looks over the proceedings from a balcony. Elsewhere, an adolescent Rogue inadvertently puts her boyfriend into a coma by making out with him, whereby we learn that (a) Rogue can extract the life force from other creatures, and (b) the mutants acquire their talents when they reach puberty. Professor Xavier has established a special school for mutants, where they can develop their abilities fully. And over the course of the film, the most mutant-phobic U.S. senator is "converted" into mutant form. In other words, the X-Men are coded as gay gifted Jewish kids with disabilities.

2 The most comprehensive discussion of literary Darwinism to date can be found in Jonathan Kramnick, "Against Literary Darwinism," and the subsequent debate among Kramnick, Paul Bloom, Brian Boyd, Joseph Carroll, Vanessa Ryan, G. Gabrielle Starr, and Blakey Vermeule in *Critical Inquiry* (2012).

3 The story goes like this. When I was four, my father took me to the main branch of the Queens Public Library, about four miles from our house. Whether I wandered off or he lost track of me, I do not know; all I know is that suddenly I could not find him anywhere. Terrified, I left the library to see whether he was on the street. There was a bus depot nearby, and I knew —at four!—that I could get home on the Q65 bus (I was always a New York City mass transit aficionado). Weirdly, however, I convinced myself that I could not take a bus because I did not have fifteen cents for the fare, forgetting that children under six ride free. At that point I began to cry, whereupon a woman

stopped and asked whether I was lost. I told her I had lost my father in the library; she asked if I knew my address and phone number (I did: 45–74 158th Street, LE9–1202). She took me back into the library, to the information desk, and had my father paged. He appeared, vastly relieved and full of gratitude for the arrival of this helpful woman (as well he should have been), and the story ended happily.

Nick never left my sight in Alderman Library.

4　In 5 *Readers Reading*, Norman Holland had argued that any reader who mistook Miss Emily for an Eskimo would be clearly misreading the text: "One would not say, for example, that a reader of . . . 'A Rose for Emily' who thought the 'tableau' described an Eskimo was really responding to the story at all—only pursuing some mysterious inner exploration" (12). In *Is There a Text in This Class?*, by contrast, Stanley Fish concedes the point but argues that the range of acceptable readings of "A Rose for Emily" is not constrained by the text itself: "The Eskimo reading is unacceptable because there is at present no interpretive strategy for producing it, no way of 'looking' or reading (and remember, all acts of looking or reading are 'ways') that would result in the emergence of obviously Eskimo readings. That does not mean, however, that no such strategy could ever come into play, and it is not difficult to imagine the circumstances under which it would establish itself" (346).

5　The Internet abounds with such speculations, as well as suggestions that Meg herself is on the Asperger's end of the spectrum. But for a brief, thoughtful consideration of the drawbacks of such diagnoses, see Stephanie Allen Crist, "Should We Label Characters?"

6　I address the implicit disability hierarchy, and the resistance of intellectual disability to processes of destigmatization, in my brief discussion of Erving Goffman's *Stigma* in "Term Paper."

7　See, for instance, the remarkable collection of essays in *Autism and Representation* (ed. Mark Osteen), Margaret Price's searing *Mad at School: Rhetorics of Mental Disability and Academic Life*, and Catherine Prendergast's terrific essay "The Unexceptional Schizophrenic: A Post-Postmodern Introduction." Osteen's introduction to *Autism and Representation* offers a particularly pointed critique of the disability hierarchy as it has been (to date) reproduced within disability studies.

8　In "The Social Model of Disability," a critique of the social model of disability, Tom Shakespeare offers a retrospective look at the movement he helped to found, and notes its reliance on the model of physical disability.

9　For representative criticisms of the episode, see David Kociemba, "'This Isn't Something I Can Fake': Reactions to *Glee*'s Representations of Disability," and S. E. Smith, "No Glee for Disabled People."

10 After submitting the manuscript of this book, I taught an undergraduate honors seminar in the fall of 2014 that drew on some of this material. One of the questions on the final exam asked students to write on the relation between intellectual disability and a character's capacity for understanding the narrative s/he inhabits. One of my students, Kassia Janesch, wrote a response that linked *Life and Times of Michael K* to Kazuo Ishiguro's *Never Let Me Go* on the grounds that Michael K and Kathy H. have so little understanding of the larger social fabric precisely because they were raised in institutions (Huis Norenius and Hailsham, respectively) whose purpose it is to prevent them from understanding the larger social fabric. Moreover, like many academic critics, Ms. Janesch traced Michael K's Bartleby-esque refusals to speak to the rules of Huis Norenius, "the twenty-one rules of which the first was 'There will be silence in dormitories at all times'" (105). Ms. Janesch argued, then, that even though Kathy H. is positively chatty compared to Michael K, she is a severely restricted narrator who is incapable of understanding the cloning/organ donation program until the chapter in which Miss Emily explains its history, and that her inability to understand her place in the scheme of things, like Michael's, is produced by the institution that disables her. This strikes me as exactly right, and suggests to me that analyses of the relation between intellectual disability and self-awareness (in characters and in texts) can go well beyond the parameters I have sketched out here.

CHAPTER 1. MOTIVE

1 For a brilliant reading of how the encounter with intellectual disability can be transformed from shock and horror into a distinctly modernist aesthetic, see Janet Lyon, "On the Asylum Road with Woolf and Mew."

2 The now-classic reading of disability in *As Good as It Gets* can be found in the introductory chapter of Robert McRuer's pathbreaking book, *Crip Theory*.

3 I discuss *Dumbo* and *Happy Feet* (as well as other thematized treatments of disability in mainstream film) in a TEDx talk, "Humans, Superheroes, Mutants, and People with Disabilities." To those observations I now have to add one from my School for Criticism and Theory seminar participant David Ferguson, who alerted me to the moment in *Wreck-It Ralph* when Vanellope von Schweetz, a character in the video game Sugar Rush, complains that she is not a glitch (a programming error in the game), but, rather, has pixlexia.

4 Indeed, Joseph N. Straus has suggested that "autism might eventually follow the path of neurasthenia and hysteria into quaintness and irrelevance," and that "this process may be hastened by the increasing incoherence of the category" ("Autism as Culture," 465).

5 *Finding Nemo, To Kill a Mockingbird,* Tiresias, *One Hundred Years of Solitude,* and *The English Patient* are Quayson's examples; the rest are mine.

6 It was a very pleasant surprise to see my work adduced by Quayson, and I believe that being assigned to the "disability as normality" category is generally a *good* thing, a sign that one has represented disability as part of the ordinary fabric of human life; though my subtitle calls Jamie an "exceptional" child, I did indeed try, throughout the book, to render his exceptionality as part of a species norm. But sometimes I wonder whether I *should* have evinced some aesthetic nervousness, in Quayson's terms. Shouldn't I be trying to disrupt the dominant protocols of something? Since it is too late to rewrite *Life as We Know It,* I will have to devote this book to that project instead.

7 See Rosemarie Garland-Thomson, "Seeing the Disabled: Visual Rhetorics of Disability in Popular Photography."

8 I am relying in part on Robert McRuer's critique of Garland-Thomson's typology in "Crip Eye for the Normate Guy: Queer Theory, Bob Flanagan, and the Disciplining of Disability Studies," in *Crip Theory:* where Garland-Thomson writes, "Realism aims to routinize disability, making it seem ordinary" (363), McRuer replies, "If we are in the realm of routinizing a particular cultural construction and making it seem ordinary, are we not potentially in the realm of ideology?" (180). (McRuer proceeds to adduce the Barthes of *Mythologies* rather than the Barthes of *S/Z,* but otherwise we are on the same page. Neither he nor I can remember which of us brought up *Paris Is Burning,* which may or may not have been adduced in the Q-and-A at the Emory conference on disability studies at which he presented the first version of this paper.)

9 I owe this point to Leon Hilton, one of my seminar participants in the School for Criticism and Theory. He did not mention smoke alarms, but he did put much-needed pressure on Quayson's "short circuit."

10 See my entry on "Disability" in *New Keywords: A Revised Vocabulary of Culture and Society,* 87–89.

11 I discuss this aspect of Searle's work in *Rhetorical Occasions* (40–41).

12 Similarly, later in the text, the narrator writes, "I thought talking and not talking made the difference between sanity and insanity. Insane people were the ones who couldn't explain themselves" (186).

13 Shklovsky, "Art as Technique"; I will return to Shklovskian moments of defamiliarization at the end of chapter 3. For a nonfictional version of this kind of narrative hyperdetail, see Cary Henderson, *Partial View: An Alzheimer's Journal,* and Henderson's description of taking his dog for a walk: "I normally go out with my little doggie twice a day. That is when she gets her

food and assimilates her food and she's ready to get rid of what's left of her food. So I go out twice a day to process my little doggie" (48).

14 I think here not only of toddler Nick angrily telling me that my not-stories were not stories, but of the screenwriting seminar in the film *Adaptation,* in which the renowned script doctor Robert McKee (played by Brian Cox) tells an auditorium of aspiring writers, "You cannot have a protagonist without desire—it doesn't make any sense, any fucking sense."

15 I owe this point to Frank Desiderio, a student in my fall 2013 undergraduate senior seminar, "More Human Than Human."

CHAPTER 2. TIME

1 In my fall 2013 senior seminar, my student Hannah Burks suggested that Benjy's eschewal of apostrophes in conjunctions (i.e., "dont") makes some of his text look like contemporary texting.

2 The film critic Andy Klein, writing in *Salon,* testifies eloquently to the difficulties of trying to reconstruct any *fabula* at all. Though he assures us that "while things may seem confusing when you first watch the film, Nolan has been very careful to make sure that, when reassembled, everything in the main part of the film—everyone's behavior and motivations—makes perfect sense," he ultimately acknowledges that there is no way to establish a *fabula* that would make sense of everything *not* in the main part of the film:

Still, even after so many viewings, after reading the script and discussing the film for months, I haven't been able to come up with the 'truth' about what transpired prior to the film's action. Every explanation seems to involve some breach of the apparent 'rules' of Leonard's disability—not merely the rules as he explains them, but the rules as we witness them operating throughout most of the film.

3 For a reading of Faulkner's Appendix that challenges Faulkner's reading of *The Sound and the Fury,* see Philip Cohen, "'The Key to the Whole Book.'"

4 I am borrowing this argument from Janet Lyon, who will eventually want it back.

5 Frank opens the essay by citing André Gide's remark that Lessing's *Laokoon,* on the relation between the visual and the literary arts, "is one of those books it is good to reiterate or contradict every thirty years" (221); the same could be said of Frank's essay, one of the touchstones of modernist criticism—written by a man who was only twenty-seven at the time. Frank does not discuss *The Sound and the Fury*; in a follow-up essay, he devotes himself entirely to Djuna Barnes's *Nightwood,* a novel he rightly considered underappreciated and that remained underappreciated for a few more decades. However, his remarks on

Ulysses can stand in very nicely for Benjy's section, and for *The Sound and the Fury* as a whole:

> Joyce cannot be read—he can only be re-read. A knowledge of the whole is essential to an understanding of any part; but, unless one is a Dubliner, such knowledge can be obtained only after the book has been read, when all the references are fitted into their proper place and grasped as a unity. Although the burdens placed on the reader by this method of composition may seem insuperable, the fact remains that Joyce, in his unbelievably laborious fragmentation of narrative structure, proceeded on the assumption that a unified spatial apprehension of his work would ultimately be possible. (234–35)

6   For a brief history of our understanding of time, see Stephen Hawking's *A Brief History of Time*. Though it is widely reputed to be the least-read bestseller of (cough) all time, it really is quite readable.

7   I owe this point—and my understanding of the term—to the savvy gamers among my School for Criticism and Theory seminar participants, Sandra Danilovic and David Ferguson.

8   A similar dynamic informs Dick's even more minor novel, *We Can Build You*, where a narrative about building lifelike android replicas of Abraham Lincoln and Edwin Stanton gradually unpacks itself as a narrative about clinical depression, partly by way of the Lincoln character.

9   At this point, SCT participant David Ferguson suggested, the novel is basically "game over," in the sense that the entire text is officially schizophrenic.

10   Quoted in Rita Kempley, "'Magic Negro' Saves the Day, but at the Cost of His Soul."

11   This line of thought was inspired, albeit obliquely, by Ian Baucom's presentation at the School for Criticism and Theory, "History 4°C: Search for a Method."

12   The challenge to the humanities was first articulated (or issued?) by Dipesh Chakrabarty, in "The Climate of History," and has been taken up with remarkable speed and energy. See, e.g., the special double issue of *Symplokē*, "Critical Climate," 21.1–2 (2013).

13   It has always puzzled me that complaints about jargon in literary criticism never focus on the field of narratology, which is nearly impenetrable to the uninitiated.

14   Perhaps the most sustained answer is that of Arthur Geffen: Dilsey's pronouncement

> surely refers to the vision she has shared with Shegog of the beginning and the end of Christ's life on earth and of two of the endpoints of Christian sacred history—the crucifixion and the judgment. . . . Her

words may then indicate that she, like Shegog, has seen God face to face. However, the statements, particularly when taken in the context in which they are later uttered, appear also to be comments on the doom of the family she has served all her life. That Dilsey is a seeress possessing intense awareness that the Compson line is dead has been commonly observed, but why does her prophetic insight emerge from the church service? Perhaps Dilsey, having moved for a time into the sacred plane of existence, can now see with utter clarity the fate of those condemned to inescapable profanity. (185)

Geffen is working with Mircea Eliade's distinction between sacred and profane time, and is emphatic about Benjy's role as the vehicle between the two. Taking off from Dilsey's claim that Benjy is "de Lawd's chile," followed by "en I be His'n too, fo long, praise Jesus" (317), Geffen writes, "on first reading, one might imagine that Dilsey's use of the term 'de Lawd's chile' refers to all human beings, all God's children. However, closer inspection proves this false, for she refers to herself as one who is not yet the Lord's child; this reward will come to her only in the afterlife. Benjy then achieves a condition on earth which she can achieve only in the other world. Clearly, Benjy's capacity for transcending profane time is a primary manifestation of his special condition" (179).

For a similar reading, see Burton, "Benjy, Narrativity, and the Coherence of Compson History": "For [Dilsey] Benjy, whom she includes among those the Lord accepts, is 'de Lawd's chile' and thus has access to an eternal rather than local view of time. . . . Her sense of Benjy's timelessness finds a visual analogue in his rapt response to Reverend Shegog's sermon on the resurrection" (217).

15 My analogy for these two endings is the strategy of the Beatles' final album, *Abbey Road*: a grand, cosmic summing-it-all-up conclusion (where "and in the end, the love you take is equal to the love you make" maps onto Dilsey's revelation) and the deliberately deflationary "Her Majesty," right down to its false final note, maps onto the final sentence of the novel.

16 I owe this point to School for Criticism and Theory seminar participant Michael Sawyer.

17 See, for the gory details, Harry Bruinius, *Better for All the World*; Steven Jay Gould, *The Mismeasure of Man*; Steven Noll, *Feeble-Minded in Our Midst*; Noll and James W. Trent, *Mental Retardation in America*; and Trent, *Inventing the Feeble Mind*.

CHAPTER 3. SELF-AWARENESS

1 I note that my discussion of narrative technique in *The Speed of Dark* is anticipated by the reader's guide itself. Specifically, I find to my surprise that I

am answering prompt number 3 of the "Reading Group Questions and Topics for Discussion":

> Lou Arrendale is the novel's main character, and most of its events are related in his voice, through his eyes. Yet sometimes Moon depicts events through the eyes of other characters, such as Tom and Pete Aldrin. Discuss why the author might have decided to write this story from more than one point of view. Do you think it was the right decision?

Allow me to pass on this question, and say simply that it was a decision that has implications for the handling of disability and narrative irony.

2　See, e.g., Osteen:

> It is difficult to accept when, given the chance to undergo an operation that will cure him of autism, Lou agrees to be normalized. . . . Is Lou behaving as his character would, or following a prescripted authorial program designed to provoke an argument or provide another recovery narrative? Because Moon is a neurotypical writer (and the mother of an autistic son), readers may suspect that her protagonist's decision is more a neurotypical wish-fulfillment than a free choice. (38)

But perhaps the point is precisely that much is lost when Lou agrees to be normalized, not least of which is his relation to Marjory, which had constituted the emotional center of the novel?

3　I assume that the references to Aristotle and Freud are self-explanatory, but for readers not immersed in literary theory, I can explain the mentions of de Lauretis and Ricoeur. I am thinking of de Lauretis's brilliant rereading of Oedipus in chapter 5 of *Alice Doesn't*, "Desire in Narrative," and Ricoeur's rereading of Freud's reading of Oedipus in "Hermeneutics: The Approaches to Symbol," particularly the observation that "Sophocles' creation does not aim at reviving the Oedipus complex in the minds of the spectators; on the basis of a first drama, the drama of incest and parricide, Sophocles has created a second, the tragedy of self-consciousness, of self-recognition" (516).

4　For more on this phenomenon, see Berger:

> Mark Haddon has said that Christopher . . . is not necessarily meant to be taken as a person with autism. The term never appears in the novel, and Haddon expressed his preference that future editions delete "autism" from their covers so that Christopher might be presented "with no labels whatsoever," either inside or outside the book (Interview). This prefer-ence is made, of course, in spite of Christopher's manifesting many of the classical or stereotypical evidences of autism. . . . We should take Haddon's comments as both true and not true, both evasive and appropriate. Christopher clearly resembles what one thinks of as a

high-functioning autistic person—as though his author had carefully
studied popular accounts of autism by Temple Grandin, Donna Williams,
Uta Frith, Simon Baron-Cohen, and Oliver Sacks and constructed
Christopher accordingly. (192–93)

5 "Nevertheless," Osteen suggests at the end of his discussion, "*Curious Incident*
is by far the best novel with an autistic character yet published, and though it
promulgates certain stereotypes, it presents autism as just another way of
being human. When I've taught the novel in undergraduate literature classes,
an initial caution not to interpret Christopher's traits as typical of all autistic
people helps to counteract the perils of stereotyping" (40).

6 Exceptions to this rule should be made for neurotypical narrators who are (a)
induced to reverie by the taste of a madeleine, (b) obsessed with their sister's
"honor," (c) Beckettian, or (d) belonging to the emperor. As I will suggest by
way of Haddon's use of Woolf later in this chapter, modernism often challenges the idea of "neurotypical" narrative regardless of whether any specific
character has an identifiable intellectual disability.

7 In *Avatar*, the obligatory magical unobtainium substance being mined on
Pandora is actually called "unobtainium." To most viewers, this may have
sounded like an especially awful piece of scriptwriting, but it is actually one of
the film's more gracious touches: "unobtainium" has been a geek joke for
decades, chiefly among SF fans and aerospace engineers. Sometimes it denotes
a rare, valuable, and expensive substance necessary for space flight; sometimes
(as in science fiction, as in *Avatar*) it is a MacGuffin that serves as a critical
element of the plot.

8 Rabinowitz summarizes these various options like so:
Mary McCarthy argued that Kinbote was really a member of the
Russian department named Botkin; Andrew Field claimed that Kinbote
had in fact been invented by Shade; and Page Stegner suggested that
perhaps, to the contrary, Shade had actually been invented by Kinbote.
Kevin Pilon wrote a chronology of *Pale Fire* as if all events—including
those in Zembla and those in Shade's poem—had really occurred. John
Stark, on the other hand, insisted that actually only "Nabokov and *Pale
Fire* (in a sense) are real; any layer inside them (actually *in* the novel) is
imagined, and none of those inside layers is more real than any other,"
although, curiously, he also criticized Shade for the realism of his
poetry . . . and praised Kinbote for a commentary that is "purely
imaginary." (122)

9 Radhika Jones's "Father-Born: Mediating the Classics in J. M. Coetzee's *Foe*"
offers an especially good reading of the role of *Roxana*.

10 I am making this up. In reality, Janet's favorite author was Woolf and mine was Joyce, so we were reasonably compatible from the start, even if her author did look down on mine. But the story tells better this way, I think.

CONCLUSION

1 My thanks to SCT participant Leon Hilton for bringing this essay to my attention.

2 See Louis Menand, "What Comes Naturally."

3 In "Re-Minding Modernism," David Herman offers a still stronger endorsement of the idea that modernism is not merely amenable but congenial to the projects of cognitive literary criticism: "Modernist narratives can both be illuminated by and help illuminate postcognitivist accounts of the mind as inextricably embedded in contexts for action and interaction" (249).

4 In his initial essay, Kramnick complains that "the recent reception of long and ambitious works by Boyd and Dutton has in the main given literary Darwinism a free pass on the science" (323), and his footnoted example is my review of Boyd in *American Scientist*. Guilty as charged, and not for a good reason, either: I severely underread Boyd's adaptationist claims and the importance attached to them. As Kramnick then proceeds to point out, Boyd, Carroll, Dutton, and company are very deliberately choosing sides in a scientific dispute, on the side of E. O. Wilson and evolutionary psychology and against Stephen Jay Gould and Richard Lewontin's critique thereof. Indeed, they tend to speak of the dispute as if it were a standoff between Rock 'Em Sock 'Em Robots in which one side simply beat down the other, as Kramnick points out in the follow-up essay:

> Fighting the fight against Gould and for Wilson is one of their major pastimes. Boyd is right that the controversy is old. That is why I quote from more recent criticism of the genetic foundations of evolutionary psychology, including those by biologists like Marcus Feldman and philosophers of science like Elizabeth Lloyd. And yet I'm not sure that anyone in the relevant fields is quite so confident that the quarrel was [as Boyd writes] "resolved within biology against Gould and in favor of adaptationism" (397). The history of science is not a tennis match. (442–43).

I regret missing this important—indeed, crucial—aspect of Boyd's work on first go, and thank Kramnick for the correction.

5 I owe this observation to Krista Quisenberry, a student in the spring 2013 graduate seminar in which we read both Boyd and Zunshine.

6 Cf. William Deresiewicz (no defender of theory he—indeed, no defender of academic criticism in any form): "I have read any number of Darwinian essays

about *Pride and Prejudice* (one critic calls it their 'fruit fly'), but I have yet to read one that told me anything interesting. The idea that the novel is about mate selection does not count as an original contribution."

7 For a devastating account of Boyd's hostility to theory and inattention to the language of texts, see Dubreuil, "On Experimental Criticism."

8 I discuss the Sokal affair and its aftermath at some length in the first three chapters of *Rhetorical Occasions*.

9 The phrase "literary competence" is a minor misstep on Kramnick's part; Boyd and Carroll took exception to it in their replies, and Kramnick withdrew it. But it harks back to an earlier moment in literary theory, at the high-water mark of structuralism, when Jonathan Culler elaborated on a form of "literary competence" analogous to that of Chomskian "linguistic competence." See Culler, *Structuralist Poetics*.

10 See Cohen's *Atlantic* essay, "Of Mice and Men: The Execution of Marvin Wilson."

WORKS CITED

Adaptation. Dir. Spike Jonze. Perf. Nicolas Cage, Meryl Streep, Chris Cooper. Columbia, 2002.

Amis, Martin. *The War against Cliché: Essays and Reviews, 1971–2000.* New York: Vintage, 2002.

Atwood, Margaret. *Surfacing.* New York: Anchor, 1972.

Augustine. *Confessions.* Harmondsworth, England: Penguin, 1961.

Avatar. Dir. James Cameron. Perf. Sam Worthington, Zoe Saldana, Sigourney Weaver. 20th Century Fox, 2009.

Bakhtin, Mikhail. *The Dialogic Imagination: Four Essays.* Edited by Michael Holquist. Translated by Caryl Emerson and Michael Holquist. Austin: University of Texas Press, 1982.

Barthes, Roland. *S/Z.* Translated by Richard Miller. New York: Hill and Wang, 1975.

Baucom, Ian. "History 4°C: Search for a Method." Lecture, School for Criticism and Theory, Cornell University, 17 June 2013.

Beckett, Samuel. *Murphy.* New York: Grove, 1957.

———. *Three Novels by Samuel Beckett: Molloy, Malone Dies, The Unnamable.* New York: Grove, 1955.

Berger, James. *The Disarticulate: Language, Disability, and the Narratives of Modernity.* New York: New York University Press, 2014.

Bérubé, Michael. "Disability." In *New Keywords: A Revised Vocabulary of Culture and Society,* edited by Tony Bennett, Lawrence Grossberg, and Meaghan Morris, 87–89. London: Blackwell, 2005a.

———. "Disability and Narrative." *PMLA* 120.2 (2005b): 568–76.

———. "Humans, Superheroes, Mutants, and People with Disabilities." TEDx talk, Penn State University, 10 October 2010. https://www.youtube.com/watch?v=w7VEMQEsy4s.

———. "Narrative and Intellectual Disability." In *Blackwell Companion to American Literary Studies*, edited by Caroline Levander and Robert Levine, 469–82. Malden, MA: Wiley-Blackwell, 2011.

———. *Rhetorical Occasions: Essays on Humans and the Humanities*. Chapel Hill: University of North Carolina Press, 2006.

———. "Term Paper." In *Profession 2010*, 112–16. New York: Modern Language Association, 2010.

Biklen, Douglas. *Autism and the Myth of the Person Alone*. New York: New York University Press, 2005.

Blamires, Harry. *The Bloomsday Book: A Guide through Joyce's "Ulysses."* London: Methuen, 1966.

Bloom, Paul. "Who Cares about the Evolution of Stories?" *Critical Inquiry* 38.2 (2012): 388–93.

Booth, Wayne. *The Rhetoric of Fiction*. Chicago: University of Chicago Press, 1961.

Boyd, Brian. "Evolution and Literary Response." In *Telling Stories: Literature and Evolution/Geschichten erzählen: Literatur und Evolution*, edited by C. Gansel and D. Vanderbeke, 64–76. Berlin: De Gruyter.

———. "For Evocriticism: Minds Shaped to Be Reshaped." *Critical Inquiry* 38.2 (2012): 394–404.

———. *On the Origin of Stories: Evolution, Cognition, and Fiction*. Cambridge: Harvard University Press, 2010.

Brooks, Peter. *Reading for the Plot: Design and Intention in Narrative*. New York: Vintage, 1985.

Bruinius, Harry. *Better for All the World: The Secret History of Forced Sterilization and America's Quest for Racial Purity*. New York: Knopf, 2006.

Burton, Stacy. "Benjy, Narrativity, and the Coherence of Compson History." *Cardozo Studies in Law and Literature* 7.2 (1995): 207–28.

Carroll, Joseph. "An Open Letter to Jonathan Kramnick." *Critical Inquiry* 38.2 (2012): 405–10.

Cervantes, Miguel. *Don Quixote*. Translated by Walter Starkie. London: Macmillan, 1957.

Chakrabarty, Dipesh. "The Climate of History." *Critical Inquiry* 35.2 (2009): 197–222.

Coetzee, J. M. *Foe*. New York: Penguin, 1986.

———. *Life and Times of Michael K*. New York: Penguin, 1983.

Cohen, Andrew. "Of Mice and Men: The Execution of Marvin Wilson." *Atlantic*, 8 August 2012. http://www.theatlantic.com/national/archive/2012/08/of-mice-and-men-the-execution-of-marvin-wilson/260713/.

Cohen, Philip. "'The Key to the Whole Book': Faulkner's *The Sound and the Fury*, the Compson Appendix, and Textual Instability." In *Texts and Textuality: Textual Instability, Theory, and Interpretation*, edited by Philip Cohen, 235–68. New York: Garland, 1997.

Conrad, Joseph. *The Secret Agent*. New York: Doubleday Anchor, 1953.

Crist, Stephanie Allen. "Should We Label Characters?" *Shift, Journal of Alternatives: Neurodiversity and Social Change*, 1 October 2010. http://www.shiftjournal.com/2010/10/01/should-we-label-characters/.

Culler, Jonathan. *Structuralist Poetics: Structuralism, Linguistics, and the Study of Literature*. Ithaca: Cornell University Press, 1975.

Davis, Lennard, ed. *The Disability Studies Reader*. 4th ed. New York: Routledge, 2013.

Defoe, Daniel. *Robinson Crusoe*. Edited by Michael Shinegal. New York: Norton, 1993.

———. *Roxana: The Fortunate Mistress*. Edited by John Mullan. New York: Oxford University Press, 2008.

de Lauretis, Teresa. *Alice Doesn't: Feminism, Semiotics, Cinema*. Bloomington: Indiana University Press, 1984.

de Man, Paul. "Semiology and Rhetoric." *diacritics* 3.3 (1973): 27–33.

Deresiewicz, William. "Adaptation: On Literary Darwinism." *Nation*, 8 June 2009, 26–31. http://www.thenation.com/article/adaptation-literary-darwinism.

Dick, Philip K. *Martian Time-Slip*. Boston: Mariner, 2012.

———. *We Can Build You*. Boston: Mariner, 2012.

Doyle, Arthur Conan. "The Naval Treaty." In *The Complete Sherlock Holmes*, 447–68. New York: Doubleday, 1986.

———. "Silver Blaze." In *The Complete Sherlock Holmes*, 335–49. New York: Doubleday, 1986.

Dubreuil, Laurent. "On Experimental Criticism: Cognition, Evolution, and Literary Theory." *diacritics* 39.1 (2009): 3–23.

Dutton, Denis. *The Art Instinct: Beauty, Pleasure, and Human Evolution*. Oxford: Oxford University Press, 2009.

Ex Parte Briseno. 135 S.W.3d 1, 2004 WL 244826 (Tex. Crim. App.).

Faulkner, William. *The Sound and the Fury*. New York: Vintage International, 1990.

Fish, Stanley. *Is There a Text in This Class? The Authority of Interpretive Communities*. Cambridge: Harvard University Press, 1982.

Flesch, William. *Comeuppance: Costly Signaling, Altruistic Punishment, and Other Biological Components of Fiction*. Cambridge: Harvard University Press, 2007.

Forster, E. M. *Aspects of the Novel and Related Writings*. London: Edward Arnold, 1974.

Foucault, Michel. "What Is an Author?" In *The Foucault Reader*, edited by Paul Rabinow, 101–20. New York: Pantheon, 1984.

Frank, Joseph. "Spatial Form in Modern Literature: An Essay in Two Parts." *Sewanee Review* 53.2 (1945): 221–40.

Friedman, C. S. *This Alien Shore*. New York: Daw, 1998.

Galaxy Quest. Dir. Dean Parisot. Perf. Tim Allen, Sigourney Weaver, Alan Rickman. DreamWorks, 1999.

Garland-Thomson, Rosemarie. *Extraordinary Bodies: Figuring Physical Disability in American Culture and Literature*. New York: Columbia University Press, 1997.

———. "Seeing the Disabled: Visual Rhetorics of Disability in Popular Photography." In *The New Disability History: American Perspectives*, edited by Paul K. Longmore and Lauri Umansky, 335–74. New York: New York University Press, 2001.

Geffen, Arthur. "Profane Time, Sacred Time, and Confederate Time in *The Sound and the Fury*." *Studies in American Fiction* 2.2 (1974): 175–97.

Godden, Richard. "Quentin Compson: Tyrrhenian Vase or Crucible of Race?" In *New Essays on "The Sound and the Fury*," edited by Noel Polk, 99–138. Cambridge: Cambridge University Press, 1993.

Goffman, Erving. *Stigma: Notes on the Management of Spoiled Identity*. New York: Simon and Schuster, 1963.

Gottschall, Jonathan. *The Storytelling Animal: How Stories Make Us Human*. Boston: Houghton Mifflin Harcourt, 2012.

Gould, Stephen Jay. *The Mismeasure of Man*. Rev. ed. New York: Norton, 1996.

Haddon, Mark. *The Curious Incident of the Dog in the Night-Time*. New York: Vintage Contemporaries, 2004.

———. "The Curiously Irresistible Literary Debut of Mark Haddon." Interview with David Welch, 2003. www.powells.com/authors/haddon.html.

Hawking, Stephen. *A Brief History of Time: From the Big Bang to Black Holes*. New York: Bantam, 1988.

Henderson, Cary. *Partial View: An Alzheimer's Journal*. Dallas: Southern Methodist University Press, 1998.

Herman, David. "Re-Minding Modernism." In *The Emergence of Mind: Representations of Consciousness in Narrative Discourse in English*, edited by David Herman, 243–72. Lincoln: University of Nebraska Press, 2011.

Holland, Norman. *5 Readers Reading*. New Haven: Yale University Press, 1995.

Homer, *Odyssey*. Translated by Richmond Lattimore. New York: Harper Perennial, 2007.

Ishiguro, Kazuo. *Never Let Me Go*. New York: Vintage, 2006.

Johnson, Barbara. "Melville's Fist: The Execution of *Billy Budd*." *Studies in Romanticism* 18.4 (1979): 567–99.

Jones, Radhika. "Father-Born: Mediating the Classics in J. M. Coetzee's *Foe*." *Digital Defoe* 1.1 (Spring 2009). http://english.illinoisstate.edu/digitaldefoe/archive/spring09/features/jones.shtml.

Joyce, James. *Ulysses*. New York: Random House, 1946.

Kempley, Rita. "'Magic Negro' Saves the Day, but at the Cost of His Soul," *Washington Post*, 7 June 2003, C1.

Kermode, Frank. *The Sense of an Ending: Studies in the Theory of Fiction*. Oxford: Oxford University Press, 1966.

Keyes, Daniel. *Flowers for Algernon*. New York: Harcourt, Brace, and World, 1966.

Kingston, Maxine Hong. *The Woman Warrior: Memoirs of a Girlhood among Ghosts*. New York: Vintage, 1975.

Klein, Andy. "Everything You Wanted to Know about *Memento*." *Salon*, 28 June 2001. http://www.salon.com/2001/06/28/memento_analysis/.

Kociemba, David. "'This Isn't Something I Can Fake': Reactions to *Glee's* Representations of Disability." *Transformative Works and Cultures* 5 (2010). http://journal.transformativeworks.org/index.php/twc/article/view/225/185.

Kramnick, Jonathan. "Against Literary Darwinism." *Critical Inquiry* 37.2 (2011): 315–47.

———. "Literary Studies and Science: A Reply to My Critics." *Critical Inquiry* 38.2 (2012): 431–60.

L'Engle, Madeleine. *A Wrinkle in Time*. New York: Farrar, Straus and Giroux, 1962.

Lévi-Strauss, Claude. *The Savage Mind*. Chicago: University of Chicago Press, 1966.

Lyon, Janet. "On the Asylum Road with Woolf and Mew." *Modernism/Modernity* 18.3 (2012): 551–74.

McRuer, Robert. "Introduction: Compulsory Able-Bodiedness and Queer/Disabled Existence." In *Crip Theory*, 1–32.

———. "Crip Eye for the Normate Guy: Queer Theory, Bob Flanagan, and the Disciplining of Disability Studies." In *Crip Theory*, 171–98.

———. *Crip Theory: Cultural Signs of Queerness and Disability*. New York: New York University Press, 2006.

Melville, Herman. *The Confidence-Man: His Masquerade*. Edited by Hershel Parker and Mark Niemeyer. New York: Norton, 2005.

———. *Moby-Dick; or, The Whale*. Edited by Hershel Parker and Harrison Hayford. New York: Norton, 1999.

Memento. Dir. Christopher Nolan. Perf. Guy Pearce, Carrie-Anne Moss, Joe Pantoliano. Columbia/Tristar, 2000.

Menand, Louis. "What Comes Naturally." *New Yorker*, 25 November 2002. http://www.newyorker.com/magazine/2002/11/25/what-comes-naturally-2.

Mitchell, David T., and Sharon L. Snyder. *Narrative Prosthesis: Disability and the Dependencies of Discourse*. Ann Arbor: University of Michigan Press, 2000.

Monk. Created by Andy Breckhman. Perf. Tony Shalhoub, Bitty Schram. USA Network, 2002.

Moon, Elizabeth. *The Speed of Dark.* New York: Ballantine, 2004.

Nabokov, Vladimir. *Pale Fire.* New York: Vintage, 1962.

Noll, Steven. *Feeble-Minded in Our Midst: Institutions for the Mentally Retarded in the South, 1900–1940.* Chapel Hill: University of North Carolina Press, 1995.

Noll, Steven, and James Trent, eds. *Mental Retardation in America: A Historical Reader.* New York: New York University Press, 2004.

Nussbaum, Martha. *Poetic Justice: The Literary Imagination and Public Life.* Boston: Beacon, 1997.

Osteen, Mark, ed. *Autism and Representation.* New York: Routledge, 2007.

———. "Autism and Representation: A Comprehensive Introduction." In *Autism and Representation,* 1–47.

Parry, Benita. "Speech and Silence in the Fictions of J. M. Coetzee." In *Writing South Africa: Literature, Apartheid, and Democracy, 1970–1995,* edited by Derek Attridge, 149–65. Cambridge: Cambridge University Press, 2000.

Pirandello, Luigi. *Naked Masks: Five Plays by Luigi Pirandello.* Edited by Eric Bentley. New York: Dutton, 1952.

Poore, Carol. "'No Friend of the Third Reich': Disability as the Basis for Antifascist Resistance in Arnold Zweig's *Das Beil von Wandsbek.*" In *Disability Studies: Enabling the Humanities,* edited by Sharon L. Snyder, Brenda Brueggemann, and Rosemarie Garland-Thomson, 260–70. New York: Modern Language Association, 2002.

Powers, Richard. *The Echo Maker.* New York: Farrar, Straus, and Giroux, 2006.

———. *Prisoner's Dilemma.* New York: Harper Perennial, 2002.

Prendergast, Catherine. "The Unexceptional Schizophrenic: A Post-Postmodern Introduction." In *The Disability Studies Reader,* 4th ed., edited by Lennard Davis, 236–45. New York: Routledge, 2013.

Price, Margaret. *Mad at School: Rhetorics of Mental Disability and Academic Life.* Ann Arbor: University of Michigan Press, 2011.

Pullman, Philip. *The Golden Compass.* New York: Knopf, 2006.

Pynchon, Thomas. *The Crying of Lot 49.* Philadelphia: Lippincott, 1966.

Quayson, Ato. *Aesthetic Nervousness: Disability and the Crisis of Representation.* New York: Columbia University Press, 2007.

Rabinowitz, Peter. "Truth in Fiction: A Reexamination of Audiences." *Critical Inquiry* 4.1 (1977): 121–41.

Ricoeur, Paul. "Hermeneutics: The Approaches to Symbol." In *Freud and Philosophy: An Essay on Interpretation,* translated by Denis Savage. New Haven: Yale University Press, 1970.

———. *Time and Narrative.* Vol. 1. Translated by Kathleen McLaughlin and David Pellauer. Chicago: University of Chicago Press, 1984.

———. *Time and Narrative.* Vol. 2. Translated by Kathleen McLaughlin and David Pellauer. Chicago: University of Chicago Press, 1985.

———. *Time and Narrative.* Vol. 3. Translated by Kathleen Blarney and David Pellauer. Chicago: University of Chicago Press, 1988.

Rowling, J. K. *Harry Potter and the Chamber of Secrets.* New York: Scholastic, 1999.

———. *Harry Potter and the Deathly Hallows.* New York: Scholastic, 2007.

———. *Harry Potter and the Goblet of Fire.* New York: Scholastic, 2000.

———. *Harry Potter and the Half-Blood Prince.* New York: Scholastic, 2005.

———. *Harry Potter and the Order of the Phoenix.* New York: Scholastic, 2003.

———. *Harry Potter and the Prisoner of Azkaban.* New York: Scholastic, 1999.

———. *Harry Potter and the Sorcerer's Stone.* New York: Scholastic, 1998.

Ryan, Vanessa L. "Living in Duplicate: Victorian Science and Literature Today." *Critical Inquiry* 38.2 (2012): 411–17.

Samuels, Ellen. *Fantasies of Identification: Disability, Gender, Race.* New York: New York University Press, 2014.

Saunders, George. "Bounty." In *Civilwarland in Bad Decline: Short Stories and a Novella,* 88–179. New York: Riverhead, 1996.

Savarese, Ralph. *Reasonable People: A Memoir of Autism and Adoption.* New York: Other Press, 2007.

Schiller, Friedrich. *On the Aesthetic Education of Man.* Translated by Reginald Snell. New York: Frederick Ungar, 1965.

Searle, John. *The Construction of Social Reality.* New York: Free Press, 1997.

Sedgwick, Eve Kosofsky. "Affect Theory and Theory of Mind." In *The Weather in Proust,* edited by Jonathan Goldberg, 144–63. Durham: Duke University Press, 2012.

———. *Epistemology of the Closet.* Berkeley: University of California Press, 1990.

Shakespeare, Tom. "The Social Model of Disability." In *The Disability Studies Reader,* 4th ed., edited by Lennard Davis, 214–21. New York: Routledge, 2013.

Shakespeare, William. *Timon of Athens.* Edited by Barbara A. Mowat and Paul Werstine. Folger Shakespeare Library. New York: Simon and Schuster, 2006.

Sheppard, Alice. "When the Saints Come Crippin' In." Unpublished paper.

Shklovsky, Viktor. "Art as Technique." In *Russian Formalist Criticism: Four Essays,* edited and translated by Lee T. Lemon and Marion J. Reis. Lincoln: University of Nebraska Press, 1965.

Siebers, Tobin. *Disability Aesthetics.* Ann Arbor: University of Michigan Press, 2010.

Smith, S. E. "No Glee for Disabled People." *Guardian,* 19 August 2010. http://www.theguardian.com/commentisfree/2010/aug/19/no-glee-for-disabled-people.

Snyder, Sharon L., Brenda Brueggemann, and Rosemarie Garland-Thomson, eds. *Disability Studies: Enabling the Humanities*. New York: Modern Language Association, 2002.

Starr, G. Gabrielle. "Evolved Reading and the Science(s) of Literary Study: A Response to Jonathan Kramnick." *Critical Inquiry* 38.2 (2012): 418–25.

Steinbeck, John. *Of Mice and Men*. New York: Penguin, 1993.

Straus, Joseph N. "Autism as Culture." In *The Disability Studies Reader*, 4th ed., edited by Lennard Davis, 460–84. New York: Routledge, 2013.

———. *Extraordinary Measures: Disability in Music*. Oxford: Oxford University Press, 2011.

Trent, James W., Jr. *Inventing the Feeble Mind: A History of Mental Retardation in the United States*. Berkeley: University of California Press, 1994.

Truchman-Tataryn, Maria. "Textual Abuse: Faulkner's Benjy." In *The Sound and the Fury: A Critical Edition*, 3rd ed., edited by Michael Gorra, 509–20. New York: Norton, 2014.

Vermeule, Blakey. *Why Do We Care about Literary Characters?* Baltimore: Johns Hopkins University Press, 2010.

———. "Wit and Poetry and Pope, or The Handicap Principle." *Critical Inquiry* 38.2 (2012): 426–30.

Wolf, Maryanne. *Proust and the Squid: The Story and Science of the Reading Brain*. New York: Harper Perennial, 2008.

Woolf, Virginia. *Mrs. Dalloway*. New York: Harcourt, 1925.

———. *The Waves*. New York: Harcourt, 1931.

Wright, David. "Mongols in Our Midst: John Langdon Down and the Ethnic Classification of Idiocy, 1858–1924." In *Mental Retardation in America: A Historical Reader*, edited by Steven Noll and James Trent, 92–119. New York: New York University Press, 2004.

Wright, Richard. *Native Son*. New York: Perennial, 1998.

X-Men. Dir. Bryan Singer. Perf. Patrick Stewart, Ian McKellan, Hugh Jackman, Famke Janssen. 20th Century Fox, 2000.

Zunshine, Lisa. *Getting Inside Your Head: What Cognitive Science Can Tell Us about Popular Culture*. Baltimore: Johns Hopkins University Press, 2012.

———. "Real Mindblindness, or, I Was Wrong." Lecture, Modern Language Association Convention, Boston, MA, 3 January 2013.

———. *Why We Read Fiction: Theory of Mind and the Novel*. Columbus: Ohio State University Press, 2006.

INDEX

ABOUT THE AUTHOR

Michael Bérubé is Edwin Erle Sparks Professor of Literature and Director of the Institute for the Arts and Humanities at Penn State University. In 2012, he served as the President of the Modern Language Association.